AT LONG LAST

THE TEXAS RANGERS' HISTORIC RUN TO THE 2023 WORLD SERIES

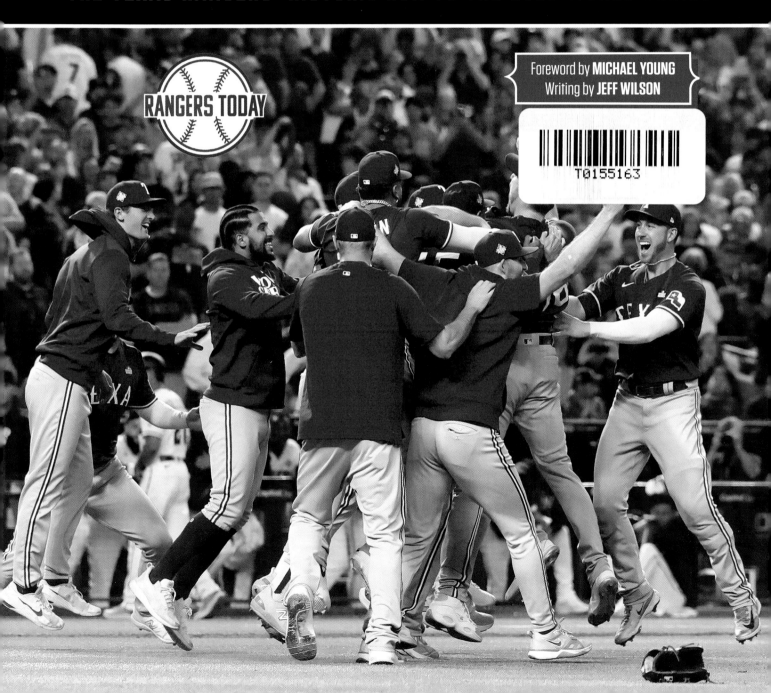

RANGERS TODAY

Foreword by **MICHAEL YOUNG**
Writing by **JEFF WILSON**

T0155163

Rangers Today would not be possible without the support of my wife, Jennifer, and children, Henry and Molly. I would be remiss in not thanking T.R. Sullivan for giving the website credibility early on and John Moore for his tireless, cheap labor. I'm grateful for our loyal and growing subscriber base that keeps this venture alive. Thanks also to the Texas Rangers, the media relations staff, Jon Daniels, Ron Washington and many others with the club past and present for helping make baseball writing my passion.

— Jeff Wilson

This book is available in quantity at special discounts for your group or organization.
For further information, contact:

Triumph Books LLC
814 North Franklin Street
Chicago, Illinois 60610
Phone: (312) 337-0747
www.triumphbooks.com

Printed in U.S.A.
ISBN: 978-1-63727-595-5

Content packaged by Mojo Media, Inc.
Joe Funk: Editor
Jason Hinman: Creative Director

Front and Back Cover Photos by AP Images

Except where otherwise noted, all interior photos by AP Images

CONTENTS

FOREWORD

By Michael Young

Texas Rangers Hall of Fame | Seven-time American League All-Star

Failing to win the World Series in 2010 and 2011 will never stop nagging me. It'll always be there. Just like if we had won it, I'd probably think about that a lot and the incredible memories. But as time goes on, I focus more on the guys I played with rather than the end result, and I appreciate every one of them. I'm just grateful for the time spent with those guys and wouldn't trade them for anything.

But nothing makes me happier than being able to say that our teams are the second- and third-best in franchise history.

The Rangers just won the World Series.

This is huge for the fans. You ask any player, and they will say that they need, that they depend on an incredibly crazy home crowd. I wish fans knew how much of a big difference it makes. I know first-hand how much they've been dying for this. At the end of the day, the game is about the players and the fans. The relationship between the two, that's how this game starts and ends.

This team did some incredible things. Going into 2011, I thought we were the best team in baseball. Ultimately, we didn't play the best. Maybe 99.9 percent of the way there we did, but it wasn't the whole way. This 2023 team did that.

When you go on the road in Houston and win Game 6 and 7 against the defending champs, against your in-state rivals, where everything was on the line and both teams know they'd never hear the end of it if they end up on the wrong end; for them to come up big and win, it becomes really, really easy to root for a team like that.

It starts at the top. Chris Young is incredibly competitive. As a special assistant in the front office and as his former teammate, I've seen a level of intensity that he had has a player that he brings to being general manager. For him, there's only one bar, and it's a championship-level bar and championship preparation. The only goal is to try to come out and win. I give him a lot of credit for that.

I can only imagine the difference manager Bruce Bochy has made for the players. When you have a manager that's done it, who's won it, there's this trust. You go in saying, "Man, this guy knows what he's doing. He's been there. He's played in the tightest moments. He's been around huge environments." You pretty much trust him right out of the gate. With Boch, he's done that times three. He's done it all.

Corey Seager and Marcus Semien have been all that the Rangers wanted when they signed them.

Everyone knew Corey could hit. You don't get a $325 million contract because you're a solid defensive shortstop. You do because you rake. But having said that, Corey is a brilliant defensive shortstop. I think he's redefining what a good shortstop is. His feet are always in the right place, he takes perfect angles, he's always ready, he's always prepared and he's incredibly intelligent. His throws are always on the money. That is what everyday shortstops have to bring.

My respect is off the charts for a guy that posts every day like Marcus Semien. He plays banged up, has had a couple stretches since he's been here where he's scuffled, and he just fights his way through it and ends up having

Manager Bruce Bochy, World Series MVP Corey Seager and the Rangers celebrate after defeating the Arizona Diamondbacks at in Game 5 to clinch the franchise's first World Series title.

huge seasons. I've got nothing but the greatest respect for that. He really is a great baseball player.

Energy guys like Adolis García are great. But he's gotten better. You don't see a lot of guys at his age where they're still improving. His plate discipline is getting better. You can see it in the way his at-bats have a tendency to unfold, where he just ends up getting himself into better counts. He can get his A swing going more often, which is going to lead to a lot more damage. It was 40 home runs for this guy, and it seems like another 40 in the postseason. And the guys love him.

Those three guys and the things that they did and the tone that they set for our club, that was a lot of fun to watch.

One thing that my Rangers teams always wanted to do was give the Metroplex its first baseball championship. For a lot of us, one reason we were so upset was because it would have been the first one.

This team had the opportunity right in front of them, and the Metroplex is one of those cities now where they can check the box that every major sport has a title. And you don't take those away, man.

Those flags fly forever. ∎

INTRODUCTION

By Jeff Wilson
Rangers Today

The history of the Texas Rangers isn't a pretty one. They came to Arlington for the 1972 season from Washington, D.C. as the second iteration of the Senators and promptly lost 100 games at the creaky Turnpike Stadium. The '73 team lost 105.

The Rangers sprinkled in some All-Star players and winning seasons over their first 24 seasons before finally reaching the postseason in 1996, 1998 and 1999. The problem was their best seasons coincided with the rise of the Yankees dynasty, and each year the damn Yankees knocked the Rangers out of the playoffs in the first round.

More mediocrity was overwritten with the franchise's first two trips to the World Series in 2010 and 2011. Neither team brought home the trophy, though the 2011 team came within one strike – twice! – of winning it all.

Fans are still scarred by that Game 6 collapse and eventual loss to the Cardinals.

Nearly 50 years after their arrival in town, the grand opening of their new $1.2-billion ballpark was nixed by a worldwide pandemic. The team the following season, in 2021, lost 102 games.

What transpired in 2023, though, should wipe away some of the pain — maybe all of it.

The Rangers have won the World Series. Finally.

They did it by beating the Arizona Diamondbacks in five games. On the way, they defeated injuries to superstars, issues with their bullpen and their No. 1 rival to be crowned as world champions for the first time.

And they went an MLB-best 11-0 on the road.

Their run to the title started in October of 2022, when general manager Chris Young coaxed manager Bruce Bochy out of semi-retirement with the chance to pursue a fourth World Series ring. He got it in Season One.

The conquering heroes were the six American League All-Stars: Corey Seager, Marcus Semien, Adolis García, Josh Jung, Jonah Heim and Nathan Eovaldi. They all did something spectacular in the 13-4 postseason run, but big contributions also came from Jordan Montgomery, Evan Carter, Mitch Garver and Jose Leclerc.

The biggest winners were the fans, some who have been on board for 51 years and others who hopped on in the 1990s and 2010s. Some didn't last long enough to see their favorite team's shining moment. Now, the fans all eagerly await the next one.

But the title also has meaning for Nolan, Pudge, Juan, Fergie, Sunny, Tom, Wash, Michael, Ian and Josh. Longtime radio voice Eric Nadel finally delivered the call of a lifetime. Ted Williams and Frank Howard might be enjoying a cool one from above. Any player who languished through all the tough seasons and the heartbreak is probably feeling a lot better today.

What follows is a chronicle of this journey, from the 2022 offseason to the best start to the regular season in franchise history; from the All-Star Game and second-half bumps in the road to the last out of the 119th Fall Classic at Chase Field in Arizona.

It was quite the ride.

The 2023 Texas Rangers are world champions at long last. ■

Manager Bruce Bochy hoists the World Series trophy. Bochy became just the sixth manager ever to win four or more World Series, and the first to do so with two different clubs.

WORLD SERIES GAME 1
October 27, 2023 • Arlington, Texas
Rangers 6, Diamondbacks 5 (11)

AGAINST ALL ODDS

Rangers Claim Spectacular Game 1 with 11th Inning Walk-Off

All that separated the Rangers from an early hole and losing home-field advantage in the World Series was two outs.

They trailed by two against a reliever who hadn't allowed a run this postseason. That reliever was facing a team that won a whopping one game in 59 tries when trailing after the eighth inning.

As bad as things looked, one ninth-inning swing changed the game. Another swing in the 11th inning might go down in the biggest in Rangers history.

Corey Seager delivered a two-run game-tying homer in the ninth, and Adolis García ended Game 1 of the 119th Fall Classic with walk-off homer that completed an improbable comeback in a 6-5 victory.

"It was a great game, entertaining game," manager Bruce Bochy said. "We had some chances out there, but couldn't quite get that big hit. But late we did. We got the big home run."

García homered for the fifth straight game, a streak that is second in MLB postseason history. He also had an RBI single in the first inning. Seager was only 1 for 4, but he walked twice and scored three times. The home run was the 10th of his career at Globe Life Field.

Evan Carter and Mitch Garver drove in a run apiece, Carter with a double after Seager walked in the first and Garver with a bases-loaded walk in the third.

But Arizona appeared to be on its way to a series-opening win.

The Diamondbacks erased an early 2-0 deficit with a three-run third inning against Rangers ace Nathan Eovaldi and added single runs in the fourth and fifth to force him out of the game. That was all they would get, though, as five relievers delivered 6 1/3 scoreless innings.

The Rangers had some opportunities after a two-run first inning but couldn't get the needed timely hit. They had runners at first and second in the eighth, but Nathaniel Lowe and Josh Jung couldn't deliver.

Arizona went to Paul Sewald for the ninth, but he walked Leody Taveras to start the inning. After striking out Marcus Semien on three pitches, Sewald tried to sneak a 93-mph fastball past Seager.

Instead, Seager launched a shot into the right-field seats and screamed his way down to first base.

"You never just want to give them a strike," Seager said. "You never want to just give them a strike. You never know if the one you're supposed to move forward is the first one, so you're just always ready." ∎

Adolis García celebrates at home plate after hitting a walk-off solo home run in the 11th inning of Game 1 in Arlington.

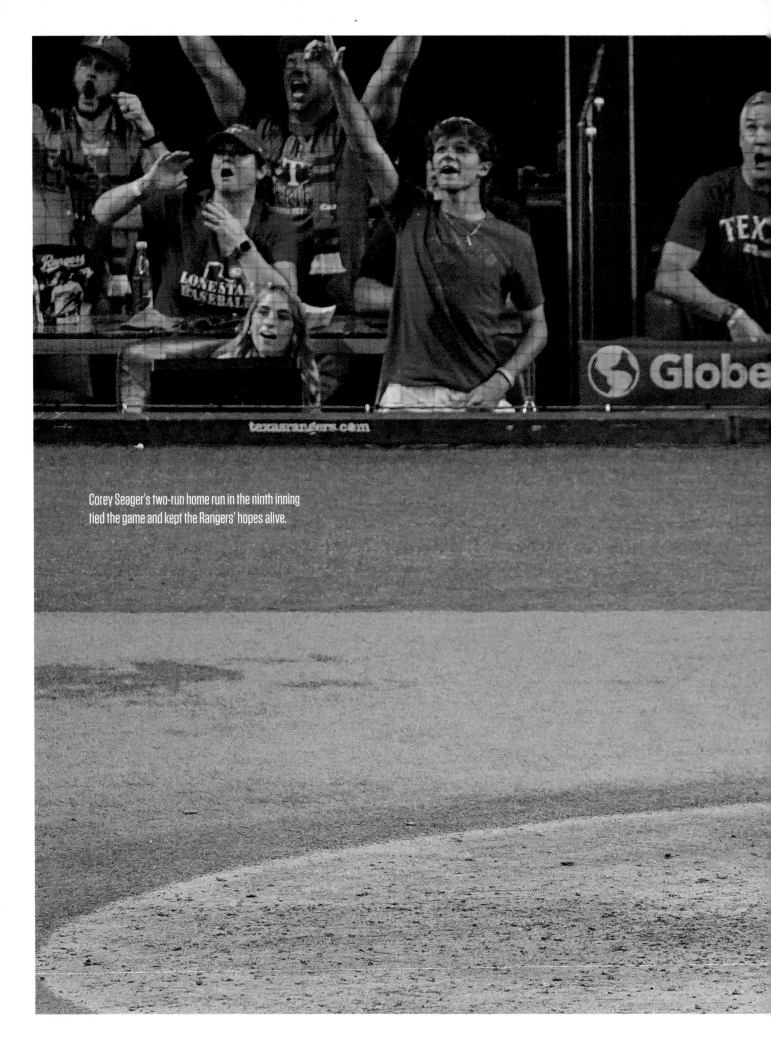

Corey Seager's two-run home run in the ninth inning
tied the game and kept the Rangers' hopes alive.

WORLD SERIES GAME 2
October 28, 2023 · Arlington, Texas
Diamondbacks 9, Rangers 1

ONE TO FORGET

Rangers Bats Stifled as Diamondbacks Roll to Easy Game 2 Win

Jordan Montgomery wasn't the best he has been all postseason, but he wasn't bad.

The Rangers' defense helped him out, turning multiple tricky rollers into outs.

Together, they gave the Rangers a chance Saturday night over the first six innings of Game 2 of the World Series.

But sometimes the other guy is just better.

Merrill Kelly allowed one run in seven innings, and Gabriel Moreno started the scoring with a fourth-inning home run as Arizona left Globe Life Field with a 9-1 victory and a spilt in the first two games of the 2023 Fall Classic.

The Diamondbacks outscored the Rangers 7-0 in the final three innings.

"It's a seven-game set," first baseman Nathaniel Lowe said. "We'd be naive to think we'd run away with four in a row. That's a team that really fights hard. It's a resilient bunch over there, but we're pretty confident in our group, too."

The series will resume at Chase Field, where Max Scherzer will be the Rangers' Game 3 starter. It's pivotal game for the Rangers, who are 8-0 on the road this postseason but were 0-2 in the regular season in Phoenix.

Mitch Garver delivered the only Rangers run with a solo homer off Kelly to start the fifth. The only other two hits he issued were broken-bat singles by Evan Carter and Josh Jung, and the Rangers didn't get their first base runner until Carter's soft liner fell in with two outs in fourth.

The Rangers finished with four hits and did not draw a walk until the ninth inning.

"It's all about execution, and pitching will always be about execution," said second baseman Marcus Semien, who singled in the ninth. "He kept it out of the middle of the zone, where we like to hit it. We're going to have to do a little bit more just to get to those pitches next time."

Arizona broke through in the fourth as Gabriel Moreno connected for a solo shot with one out and as Lourdes Gurriel Jr. delivered a two-out single that scored Tommy Pham after the second of his four hits.

But Arizona lead only 2-1 when Montgomery came back for the seventh inning. He issued a double and a single, leading to the third Arizona run, and that was it for the left-hander. Though he threw only 75 pitches, Montgomery surrendered nine hits and did not record a strikeout, which might suggest he hadn't fully recovered from his relief outing in Game 7 of the American League Championship Series.

His velocity was down slightly.

"I don't know how much it affected him, but he's not saying it did," manager Bruce Bochy said. "You look at the man. He's got the ability to pitch if it's down a tick, and he showed that tonight."

Emmanuel Rivera scores during the eighth inning as catcher Jonah Heim handles the throw. The Diamondbacks outscored the Rangers 7-0 in the final three innings.

The Diamondbacks scored two more in the seventh, both charged to Montgomery, and tallied three in the eighth and two in the ninth to put the game out of reach.

Kelly, though, took the starch out of the Rangers' bats and the capacity crowd of 42,500. He struck out nine and didn't issue a walk, and he limited the first four Rangers batters — Semien, Corey Seager, Carter and Adolis Garcia — to one hit in 12 at-bats.

"A lot of his pitches look really similar," first baseman Nathaniel Lowe said. "He's just had it going tonight. He wasn't missing a lot of spots, he was on the edge, he was ahead in the count, and that's how you pitch."

The Rangers are traveling Saturday to Phoenix, and they will hold an evening workout at Chase Field. They have until 7:03 p.m. Monday to put their Game 2 loss behind them.

"Every single loss in the big leagues, that's definitely the plan," Semien said. "It is a World Series this loss and nobody wants to be in this situation, but what else can you do? We have a day off to rejuvenate the bodies and come back strong." ■

WORLD SERIES GAME 3
October 30, 2023 · Phoenix, Arizona
Rangers 3, Diamondbacks 1

IN THE MOMENT
Rangers Take Game 3, But Questions Remain

Bruce Bochy worries about tomorrow tomorrow. The only thing on his mind is winning the game directly in front of him.

The Rangers manager is a tough one to doubt, with three World Series rings and more than 2,000 regular-season wins.

On Monday, Game 3 of the World Series stood before the Rangers.

They won it over the Diamondbacks, 3-1, and took a 2-1 lead on the best-of-7 series.

Here are the highlights:

Jon Gray was terrific over three scoreless innings out of the bullpen.

"Did a terrific job, didn't he?" Bochy said.

Marcus Semien drove in the game's first run with a two-out single in the third.

Corey Seager followed with a two-run homer.

"I think they showed what they mean to us with their outstanding play," Bochy said.

Adolis García threw out Christian Walker at home plate in the second to keep the game scoreless.

Evan Carter, the rookie who didn't make his MLB debut until Sept. 8, batted fourth and singled twice and walked.

"Double-A feels like a couple of years ago," he said.

Seager made the defensive play of the game has he sild/dived to his left and made backhanded toss to Semien to trigger a double play that ended the eighth inning with Arizona rallying.

"Tremendous job on Marcus' part, especially with that transfer in the turn," Seager said. "What he did really made that play. It was a big momentum change for us, for sure."

However, it wasn't easy. And things aren't going to get any easier.

García left the game in the eighth inning with tightness in his left side. He grabbed at it after his final swing of his inning-ending at-bat and after the game was sent to an area MRI machine.

"We're being optimistic there, but we'll know more tomorrow," Bochy said.

Max Scherzer left after three scoreless innings with back spasms. He said after the game that the back was still in lockdown and he wouldn't know until Wednesday if he will be able to pitch again in the series.

"Same with Max," Bochy said.

The biggest concern is with García, the MVP of the American League Championship Series and the hero of

Corey Seager hits a two-run home run during the third inning of Game 3. Seager's heroics at the plate were matched by his defensive play, shutting down a potential Diamondbacks rally later in the game.

Game 1 of the 119th Fall Classic thanks to a walk-off homer in the 11th inning.

If he is unable to play in Game 4, Robbie Grossman would likely play right field. If García is unable to play the rest of the series, the Rangers could activate utility player Ezequiel Duran. They would really make a splash by adding first-round pick Wyatt Langford, who has been staying active as part of a mini-camp in Arlington.

"He's been the heart and soul of our team," Semien said of García. "That being said, we've had Adolis go down earlier this season. We've had guys step up."

That's been the story of the Rangers' season, with Duran replacing Seager early in the season, Dane Dunning replacing Jacob deGrom and Carter replacing García.

The Rangers are now two wins away from winning their first World Series, but all that matters to Bochy is the game in front directly of him.

Winning Game 4 won't be easy, but not much has been for the Rangers the past two months. ■

Above: Marcus Semien drives in the game's first run with a two-out single in the third inning. Opposite: Starting pitcher Max Scherzer pitched three scoreless innings before exiting the game with back spasms.

WORLD SERIES GAME 4
October 31, 2023 · Phoenix, Arizona
Rangers 11, Diamondbacks 7

ALL THE RIGHT MOVES

Semien, Seager Power Rangers to Game 4 Win, Cusp of World Title

A popular word used to describe the 2023 Texas Rangers has been "resilient," and, sure enough, they've shown an uncanny ability to endure hard times throughout their first winning season since 2016.

And hours before Game 4 on Tuesday presented some hard times.

Adolis García and Max Scherzer were deemed too injured to participate in the World Series again. You know, the American League Championship Series MVP and a three-time Cy Young winner.

And, yes, the Rangers didn't seem to let adversity bother them in Game 4.

But instead of resilient, how about saying they're just really good?

The Rangers scored five times in the second and third innings, buoyed by home runs from Corey Seager and Marcus Semien, and an 11-7 victory moved them within one win of capturing their first World Series.

They lead the best-of-7 series 3-1 after improving to 10-0 on the road this postseason and have a chance to clinch Wednesday night in Game 5, with postseason ace Nathan Eovaldi on the mound against Diamondbacks ace Zac Gallen in a rematch of Game 1.

"We don't want to mess around tomorrow," first baseman Nathaniel Lowe said. "We saw it today in the late innings: They're not going to give up. Gallen's got his back against the wall. It's win or go home. We'd be stupid to think that they just going to roll over and just give us this fourth win. But we'd be selling ourselves short not to be confident."

The Rangers took leads of 10-0 and 11-1, which served as plenty of cushion as Arizona mounted rallies in the eighth and ninth innings against the Rangers' lower-leverage relief arms. Jose Leclerc was summoned for the final out instead of getting a day off.

It looked like he wouldn't be needed after the Rangers scored their first 10 runs with two outs. Jonah Heim led off the eighth with a home run for the Rangers' final tally.

Josh Jung, up in the order to fifth with García (oblique strain) out, opened the second inning with a double and was at third with two outs when Miguel Castro uncorked a wild pitch that got just far enough away for Jung to score the game's first run.

Leody Taveras then walked, and Travis Jankowski, playing right field for García, followed with a single. Semien was next, and he tripled into the left-field corner for a 3-0 lead. Seager followed that with a drive to deepest part of Chase Field.

With a triple in the second inning and a home run in the third, Marcus Semien led the Rangers with 5 RBIs in Game 4.

Jung and Lowe singled with one out in the third, and everyone was safe as Arizona first baseman Christian Walker bobbled a Heim chopper. Taveras struck out, but Jankowski doubled in two runs and Semien lofted his first homer of the postseason just over the left-field wall.

"We just had some guys that had some really nice days," manager Bruce Bochy said. "I mean Marcus and Corey, and, of course, Jankowski. Really a lot of guys did some good things there tonight."

Left-hander Andrew Heaney was the beneficiary of the run support, and he opened with three scoreless innings. Arizona get on the board in the fourth, but Heaney returned for a scoreless fifth before giving way to Dane Dunning.

Seager said that Heaney was the hero of the game. While the Diamondbacks threw a bullpen game, the Rangers were potentially in a similar situation, but Heaney got them deeper in the game that perhaps even they were anticipating.

Five runs in the second inning there really takes a lot of pressure off," he said. Then putting up five the very next inning, we had a 10-run lead, and it's a lot easier to go out there attack the strike zone and not feel so confined to having to make perfect pitches."

Dunning and Cody Bradford worked a scoreless inning apiece in the sixth and seventh before Arizona scored four in the eighth against Brock Burke, who replaced Scherzer on the roster, and Chris Stratton.

Will Smith allowed the first two runners to reach against Will Smith, who gave way with two outs to Leclerc. He allowed a two-run single to Gabriel Moreno, but got Christian Walker to end it and move the Rangers to the cusp of becoming world champions.

"You can't take anything for granted," Seager said. "They're a good team. They're going to scrap, they're going to claw and they're never going to give up. They showed that today. We've got to come ready to play." ∎

Travis Jankowski contributed to the Rangers' early scoring with a two-run double. Jankowski started in right field in place of the injured Adolis García, who motivated his teammates with a speech during the pre-game hitters meeting.

WORLD SERIES GAME 5
November 1, 2023 • Phoenix, Arizona
Rangers 5, Diamondbacks 0

WENT AND TOOK IT!

Rangers Shut Down Diamondbacks, Claim First World Series Crown in Franchise History

For many, 1972 was a lifetime ago. That was when the Rangers relocated to Arlington, Texas.

Even 2011, when the Rangers couldn't close out the Fall Classic, seems like the distant past.

All previous heartbreak from the previous 52 seasons vanished Wednesday night.

Go crazy, folks: The Texas Rangers are — finally! — World Series champions.

Nathan Eovaldi gave the Rangers a chance in Game 5 with six scoreless innings, Mitch Garver broke a scoreless tie in the seventh inning against a masterful Zac Gallen and Marcus Semien capped a four-run ninth inning with a two-run homer that sent the Rangers to a 5-0 victory and their first world title.

The Rangers, who were doubted after losing the final game of the season and missing out on the American League West title, went 11-0 on the road in the postseason.

"We just came together at the right time," first baseman Nathaniel Lowe said. "It's out of our control what can happen, but this group never gave up. We got ourselves in a position to contend, and we did it the hard way. We showed up here and executed when we needed to."

Shortstop Corey Seager was selected as the Willie Mays MVP for the second time in his career. Half of his six hits in the series were home runs, and his first hit Wednesday ended six no-hit innings by Diamondbacks ace Gallen.

"This is nothing other than winning games," Seager said. "It doesn't matter who the guy is, how you do it. When it comes down to the World Series, it's about winning four games, and that's what we did."

The Rangers didn't get to celebrate, though, without the performance by Eovaldi, who delivered a gritty effort that saw him dodge trouble throughout. He and two relievers combined on the five-hit shutout.

Eovaldi was dealing with base runners from the first batter he faced, as leadoff hitter Corbin Carroll walked on four pitches. Carroll advanced to first with one out, but Eovaldi wiggled out of the jam.

He worked around a leadoff single in the second, kept the game scoreless in the third after the Diamondbacks had runners at second and third with one out and wasted a two-out double in the fourth.

The Diamondbacks kept the pressure on in the fifth, loading the bases with two outs. Lourdes Gurriel Jr.,

Pitcher Josh Sborz and catcher Jonah Heim embrace on the mound after Sborz struck out Arizona's Ketel Marte to record the final out of Game 5. Sborz recorded the final seven outs.

though, bounced the first pitch he saw to Seager, who threw across for the final out.

"I just didn't do a very good job of executing my pitches until I needed to," said Eovaldi, who went 5-0 this postseason in six starts. "The lead-off walk to start the game, having traffic, it wasn't easy. And I was able to make the big pitches when I really needed to."

Meanwhile, Gallen was cruising, though Lowe drew a two-out walk in the fight to become the Rangers' first base runner and Gallen threw 24 pitches in the inning.

Eovaldi and Gallen exchanged 1-2-3 innings in the sixth, and Gallen was at only 72 pitches when he returned for the seventh. Seager, though, singled to start the inning, breaking up the no-hit bid, and Evan Carter followed with a double.

Garver was next, and his grounder through the middle brought in the game's first run.

"I swung at the first-pitch curveball and got a good swing off," he said. "I think he wanted to challenge me with the heater, and he threw it right down the middle."

Then, it was nail-biting time, as if the first six innings hadn't frayed most fans' nerves.

Aroldis Chapman and Josh Sborz combined on a scoreless seventh. After the Rangers missed a scoring chance in the eighth, Sborz returned for a scoreless bottom half to set the stage for the ninth inning.

Josh Jung opened with a single and went to second as Lowe also singled. Heim followed with a third straight single that Alek Thomas misplayed, allowing the ball to go to the center-field wall as two runs scored.

After Leody Taveras struck out, Semien launched his second postseason homer.

"You show up every day because you never know when you're going to do something special," said Semien, who also homered, tripled and drove in five runs in Game 4.

Sborz stayed in for the ninth and easily mowed through three Arizona hitters. When Ketel Marte struck out looking, the Rangers' dugout and bullpen flooded onto the field for the biggest celebration in franchise history.

The team that lost 102 games two seasons ago became the quickest team in MLB history to win a World Series after losing 100 games. Manager Bruce Bochy, who won his fourth World Series, credited general manager Chris Young and ownership for turning the franchise around.

"I am very fortunate, blessed, to come into this. It's such a great group of guys," Bochy said. "But it starts at the top. Those guys were committed. And, look, we're in a good place now." ■

Mitch Garver celebrates his seventh-inning RBI single, which drove in Corey Seager and finally opened the scoring.

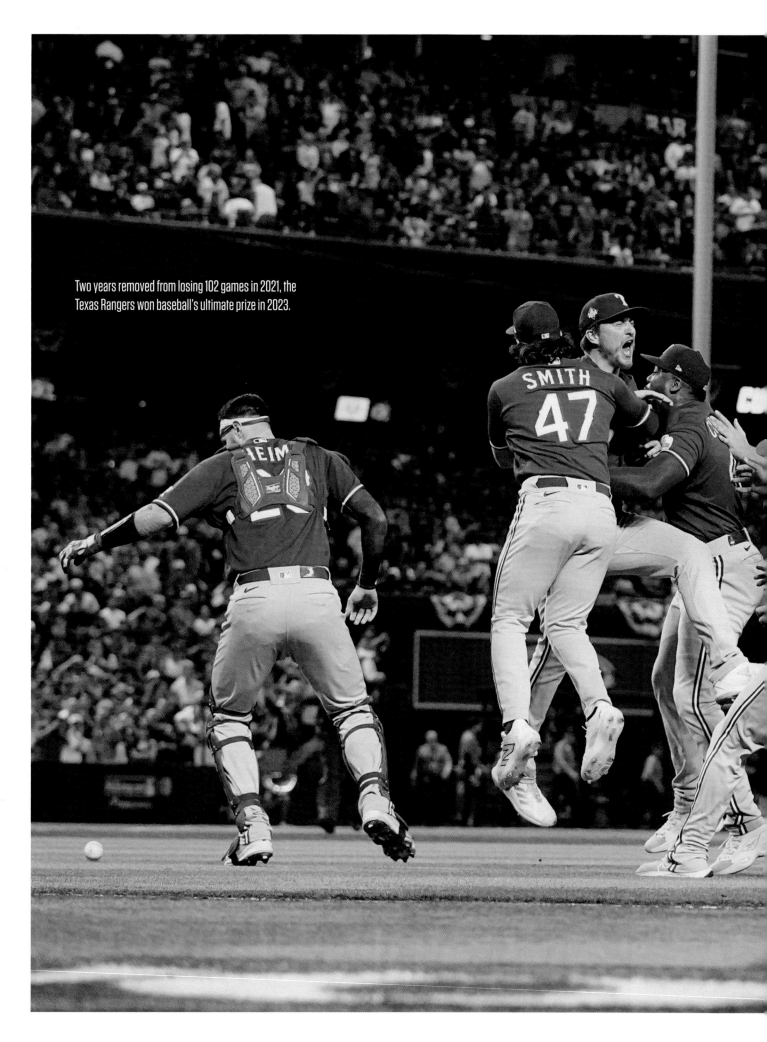

Two years removed from losing 102 games in 2021, the Texas Rangers won baseball's ultimate prize in 2023.

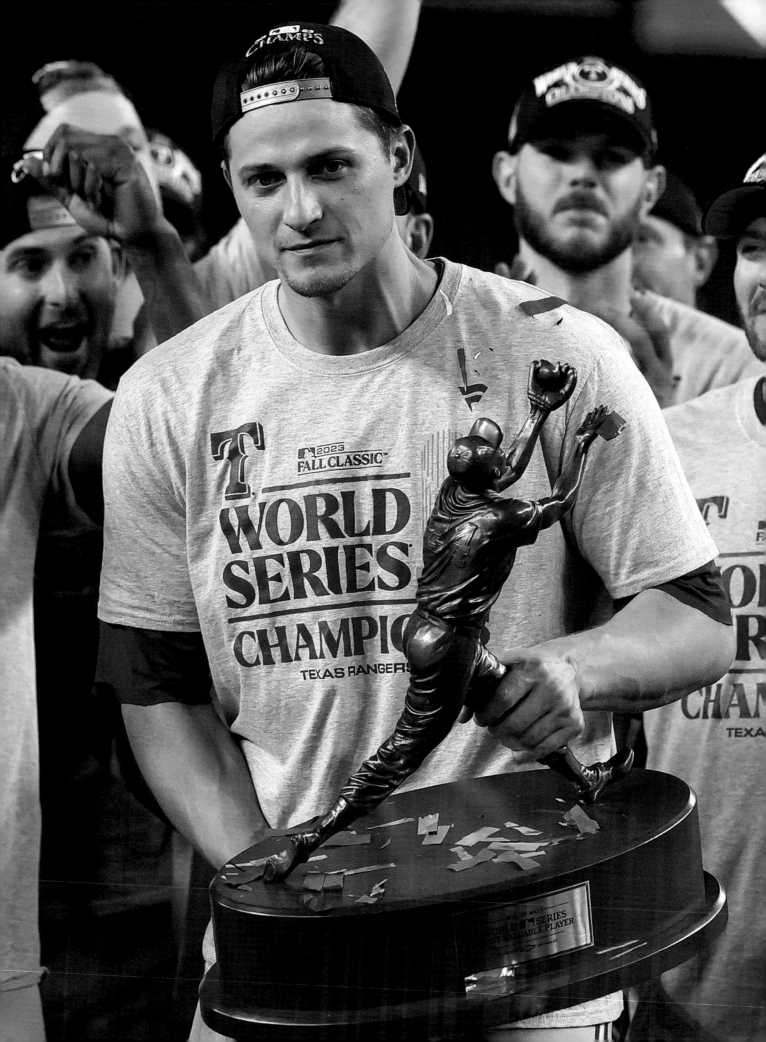

THE LAST LAUGH

Critical Home Runs Made Corey Seager Easy Choice for World Series MVP

Corey Seager had never missed the MLB postseason when he hit free agency after the 2021 season. In 2020, he won the World Series with the Dodgers and was the series MVP.

But he left it all behind Dec. 1, 2021, for a pretty penny but also because he was sold on the vision that the Texas Rangers, who had just lost 102 games and hadn't sniffed the postseason for a half-decade, would soon be world champions.

He was doubted, of course, and labeled as having sold his soul for a 10-year, $325 million contract.

Somewhere in the spray from hundreds of Budweisers and champagne bottles Wednesday night, he had the last laugh.

Seager's single to start the seventh inning of Game 5 sparked the offense, which scored five times in the final three innings after being no-hit for the first six, and the Rangers pulled away for a 5-0 victory that clinched the franchise's first World Series.

Seager was named the Willie Mays MVP, though not so much for ruining Zac Gallen's chance at history. Seager's home runs in Games 1, 3 and 4 changed the course of all three games, and without them the Rangers wouldn't have won the series in five games.

The award was the second of his career, a feat accomplished only three other times by some of the biggest names in baseball — Sandy Koufax, Bob Gibson and Reggie Jackson.

"I don't think you can ever fathom that," he said. "It's a pretty special group to be part of."

Seager batted .286 (6 for 21) but with a 1.137 OPS. He bailed the Rangers out of two-run Game 1 deficit with a ninth-inning blast that tied the game. His homer in Game 3, another two-run shot, provided the final tallies in a 3-0 win, and his Game 4 homer capped a five-run second inning that took the starch out of the Chase Field crowd.

"But it's not just me, man," Seager said. "What this team did and how we competed and all the guys in there rallying, we don't really have one leader. That whole clubhouse is the leadership. They're all professionals in there, and we all knew we had a job and task at hand. And we competed and we did it. It's pretty cool."

The championship was the realization of the vision the Rangers presented to Seager during their courtship of him as a first-time free agent. The money helped, sure, but general manager Chris Young and former top executive Jon Daniels showed Seager their blueprint.

It might have come together more quickly than anyone envisioned that day, and the window for the Rangers to be perennial contenders is just opening.

"I won in LA. They hadn't won in 30 years, and I saw what it did to a fan base," Seager said. "When I found out they had never won here, that was something that intrigued me, to be able to start at the bottom and try and build something and compete. To be able to do it, it's really satisfying.

"But it was a lot of trust, a lot of trust from them to me and me to them. It's pretty cool to see it through." ■

Corey Seager became only the fourth player to win two World Series MVPs, capturing the honor after delivering crucial home runs in Games 1, 3 and 4 against Arizona.

ROAD TO THE POSTSEASON

IT STARTS AT THE TOP

Following Bochy Hire, Maddux Returns to Texas in Leadership Shakeup
November 27, 2022

If the MLB offseason were based strictly on coaching hires and front-office additions, the Rangers would have already won it.

Convincing manager Bruce Bochy to return to the game is widely viewed as a game-changer. Dayton Moore agreeing to serve as a special advisor for baseball operations, and someone to mentor general manager Chris Young, is another significant move.

And so is the return of pitching coach Mike Maddux, announced on the same Thanksgiving Eve press release as Moore's addition but deserving of its own headline.

If not for Bochy, Maddux would top the marquee.

Here's why: The Rangers have been to the playoffs only once since Maddux wasn't kept on after the 2015 season, but six of Maddux's past seven teams have reached the postseason. He oversaw Rangers pitchers during the World Series seasons, and later watched Max Scherzer win back-to-back Cy Young awards with Washington.

St. Louis wanted Maddux back after their fourth straight postseason trip, but, truth be told, he wasn't entirely sure he wanted to be a full-time pitching coach.

He wanted to be near his Tarrant County home more than just in the offseason, and the Rangers' job might have been the only one he would have taken.

Maddux is still considered one of the best pitching coaches in the game, and his voice will be the strongest the Rangers have had since, well, he was pushed out.

"Mike has a tremendous track record as a successful pitching coach in the major leagues, and he's obviously been the most successful pitching coach in Rangers history, in my opinion," Young said. "And I think that all of his attributes and his skill set are going to serve us extremely well."

SITUATION AT HAND

Maddux replaces co-pitching coaches Doug Mathis and Brendan Sagara and is inheriting a pitching staff that is a work-in-progress. The Rangers are still attempting to upgrade via free agency or trade, and roles in the bullpen are wide open.

The Rangers are also still trying to exit their latest rebuild mode. So were the Rangers in 2009 when they hired Maddux away from Milwaukee.

The Rangers went to the World Series for the first time the next season.

As was also the case in 2009, a former pitcher is now overseeing baseball operations. Young and Nolan Ryan differed as pitchers, but their philosophy seems to have struck a chord with Maddux.

While Maddux then formed a tight bond with relatively inexperienced manager Ron Washington, he now gets the supremely experienced Bochy.

Mike Maddux previously oversaw Rangers teams that reached the World Series in 2010 and 2011. His return to the team was announced a month after Bruce Bochy became the Rangers' new manager.

"There's a comfort level with Boch," Young said. "And I think that both of them have an alignment and philosophically are in agreement with the way they see the game. And I think that's extremely important, that continuity and alignment between the manager and the pitching coach."

Maddux said that he spoke only once with Bochy during the Rangers' courtship, but that was all that was needed. It took only one conversation with Young to get Maddux interested in continuing to serve as a pitching coach.

There's some old-school in Young and Maddux, even though their only previous encounter was Maddux phoning Young after the 2014 season to recruit him to the Rangers. They believe in the eye test, starters working deep into games and pitchers being ready for every game and scenario.

"It definitely was one of our common threads that we found out right away when we were just having a baseball discussion," Maddux said. "And it was very refreshing that pitching is more than numbers. It's about attitude and fortitude, manage what we're doing. The intangibles, the unmeasurable things, are big, and those are high priorities for both of us."

COACHING STYLE

That does not mean that Maddux ignores analytics. No one does these days. As Bochy said at his introductory press conference, he wants all the information he can get to help the Rangers win.

Numbers are part of pitching, Maddux said, but can't be the only way to pitch.

"There's room for analytics to help everybody," he said. "I think there's room for baseball acumen to help people. It takes information, which is analytics, and it takes wisdom, which is coaching, and it's a blend of the two."

Young has said that the Rangers are building a pitching department that will have a wide array of baseball people. Sagara, who many Rangers pitchers leaned on for

data, is expected to be part of it as he takes on a new role.

Maddux's best attribute, Young said, is his ability to instill confidence and pitch with conviction. Maddux was Holland's first pitching coach and helped the young left-hander learn the big-league ropes and instilled the confidence in him to excel in big moments such as Game 3 of the 2010 American League Championship Series and Game 5 of the 2011 World Series.

"Committing to each pitch is one of his big things," said Holland, a free agent who would welcome a reunion with Maddux and the Rangers.

"Trusting yourself is the hardest thing to do in this game, and he reminds you of that while teaching you to trust the stuff you have. He's great with the guys, and knows how to relate to each individual pitcher. Focus is key with him, and will continue to help you improve each time you are out there."

Past pitchers under Maddux, from Holland to Cardinals veteran Adam Wainwright, have raved about his ability to break down an opposing lineup.

That's where the eye test and the data might differ. A batter might hit .350 against, say, left-handed breaking balls, but for the past week he's looked foolish on them. Pitchers trust Maddux's scouting reports.

"He taught me so much about how to pitch and scouting," Holland said. "He knows the game so well and cares about his players and their craft. He's the old-school type of mentality with teaching how to pitch and getting guys to go the distance. I'm sure he incorporates the analytics, but his main philosophy is to throw strikes and pitch your game."

Above all, Maddux said, Rangers pitchers are going to pitch from a point of strength and be prepared.

"We've got to hold them accountable to preparation," he said. "And that accountability is a big thing. Players owe their teammates to be prepared. I will make sure they are." ■

General Manager Chris Young believes that Bruce Bochy and pitching coach Mike Maddux share similar philosophies, mixing old-school wisdom with newer analytics.

EYE ON THE PRIZE

Nathan Eovaldi Chose Rangers to Win Championships
January 5, 2023

The Texas Rangers, the not-so-proud possessors of six straight sub-.500 records, introduced the latest addition to their starting rotation by saying that right-hander Nathan Eovaldi wants to win championships in this new phase of his career.

Championships and the Rangers haven't been in the same sentence often throughout the years.

Here's one: The Rangers have never won a World Series championship.

Eovaldi won one in 2018 with the Red Sox, whom he left in order to sign a two-year, $34 million deal to play in his home state.

And to win championships. The Rangers, he said, have the foundation to do so.

"I think it's about the way the ownership's been going to build an organization from the ground up," Eovaldi said. "It takes more than just the 25-man and 40-man guys. It takes the entire organization, and I feel that they want to win. It starts with this season."

He's a steadfast believer that quality starting pitching wins championships. He joins a rotation that includes newcomers Jacob deGrom, Andrew Heaney and former teammate Jake Odorizzi, who could slide into a swing role in which he makes 10 starts in 2023 while serving as a key member of the bullpen.

Martin Perez and Jon Gray are 2022 holdovers, and Dane Dunning and Glenn Otto appeared to be ticketed as rotation depth in the minors.

A good rotation makes the bullpen better, which makes the team better. The lineup doesn't feel pressure to score eight runs to win a game, which makes the hitters better.

"It makes the whole thing better," general manager Chris Young said.

Eovaldi is going to pitch for Team USA in the World Baseball Classic during spring training. He said he is already throwing bullpen sessions and feels great. He was limited to only 20 starts in 2022 because of back and shoulder injuries, but he finished fourth in American League Cy Young voting in 2021.

He continues the Rangers' offseason trend of identifying pitchers who limit walks while striking out hitters at an above-average clip. He said he would rather have one-pitch outs than strikeouts but with his five-pitch arsenal feels confident that he will pick up an out as long as he jumps ahead early in counts.

"The hitters have to earn their way on base," Young said. "It certainly was a focal point for us in terms of our offseason targets in the area that we've dramatically needed to improve. And I think we've addressed that in terms of the pitchers that we have this offseason."

Nathan Eovaldi had championship ambitions when he joined the Rangers, despite the franchise's recent woes.

Eovaldi is also excited to be pitching in Texas. A product of Alvin High School, the same school that produced Nolan Ryan, Eovaldi lives in the Houston area and said that the short commute to Arlington will make life easier on his wife and two young kids, and him, too.

Everyone is happier when they are with their family. Geography factored into his decision on where to sign.

"I mean, it's everything," he said. "I think one of the biggest things is family."

Eovaldi has a new baseball family now, and he's aiming to win championships with it. ■

Opposite: Adolis García greets starting pitcher Nathan Eovaldi before a regular-season game against the Detroit Tigers. Above: Eovaldi addresses reporters during World Series media day.

6

THIRD BASE

....

JOSH JUNG

Despite Hot Start, Rangers' Rookie is 'Never Satisfied'
May 2023

Of all the players the Rangers acquired the past two offseasons, either via trade or free agency, none of them was a third baseman.

They had their guy, an oft-injured former first-round pick from Texas Tech.

The Rangers didn't budge last offseason after watching the heir apparent to the position strike out 39.7 percent of the time in his first stint in the major leagues.

"I've never struck out like that in my life," Josh Jung said.

The Rangers stuck with the player they selected with the eighth overall pick in 2019, the year after Adrian Beltre retired. They had little success with finding a suitable replacement for Beltre, though Hall of Fame players don't come along very often.

Jung is no Beltre, but he is more productive than Asdrubal Cabrera, Isiah Kiner-Falefa, Brock Holt, Andy Ibanez, Yonny Hernandez and Charlie Culberson were in trying to replace Beltre.

Jung has enjoyed two solid months to begin his first full season in the major leagues, producing at the plate and playing solid defense at a position that hasn't been the same since Beltre stepped away in 2018.

Josh Jung made an impression early in the 2023 season, winning AL Rookie of the Month in both April and May.

"Josh has been tremendous," general manager Chris Young said. "He's just done exactly what we thought he's due, and maybe more so. The room for him to continue to get better and improve is extremely high."

Jung is in the conversation for American League Rookie of the Year, and his campaign got off to a fast start. He was selected as the AL Rookie of the Month for April after hitting .270 with six home runs, five doubles and 21 RBIs in 26 games. He finished with a .500 slugging percentage as the Rangers' No. 5 hitter behind Adolis García.

The six home runs were a club record for a rookie at the end of April, breaking García's 2021 mark of five, and the 21 RBIs were a record by a Rangers rookie, shattering David Murphy's record of 16 in 2008.

Jung led all AL rookies in RBIs, slugging percentage and runs (18), and tied for first in homers, hits (27), doubles (5). His batting average ranked second.

Yet, Jung was surprised that he was chosen as the top rookie by media who cover the league.

"I didn't feel like I had a great month," he said. "I knew I hit some homers. I was hitting like .270 or something at that point, but to me, it was like, man, there's so much room for growth within that month.

"To win that award was just crazy because I feel like I could have done way better and my best version would have done a way better than the numbers I put up."

Jung went through a rough stretch in early May, when he went 3 for 26 to drop his average from .275 to .244. Through May 15, he had struck out 52 times on the season and drawn only eight walks, but he was starting to trend the right way.

"I have a good couple of games and I have a rough stretch and I have a good couple of games," Jung said. "It's just been up and down for me so far, so it's just trying to find that consistency, trying to tinker every day to try to figure out the best version of myself. I still feel like we're trying to get there."

Rangers hitting coaches Donnie Ecker and Tim Hyers, as well as minor-league hitting coordinator Cody Atkinson, regularly give Jung feedback on his swing.

Together, they identified a mechanical flaw in Jung's stride that was leading to some of his May issues.

"Now, it's about getting everything synced back up," he said.

He believed that cleaning that up would allow him to chase some individual goals: batting .300, trimming his strikeouts and increasing his walks.

To do that, though, he said he has to stay in the moment. The more he plays, the thicker the scouting report on him gets, so he can never think he has things figured out.

"For me, it's put myself in the best position at the plate to be adjustable where I need to be," Jung said. "And that's what I'm trying to figure out. I feel like last year I got away from it a little bit, and it's kind of been a lost art to me for a while.

"So it's just like putting my ego to the side and saying, 'Hey, if I go up and I get out four times today, it doesn't matter as long as I am being stubborn and I'm making a move I want to make in the long run."

Even though he's not satisfied with his performance, he acknowledges that he's in a much better place than he was in September 2022 when the Rangers promoted him for his major-league debut.

He connected for a home run in his first career at-bat, joining Jurickson Profar in 2012 as the only players in Rangers history to do that, but he batted only .204 in his first taste of the big leagues and struck out 39 times in 98 at-bats.

Jung admitted that he was pressing at the plate after missing much of the season because of shoulder surgery

Although he suffered a late-season thumb fracture which kept him out of action for over a month, Josh Jung was able to return to the Rangers in time for their momentous playoff run.

just before spring training. It was the second straight spring that he had a significant injury that delayed his season.

The 2022 injury, though, might have prevented him from winning the starting job for Opening Day, and that made the early portion of his rehab more mentally taxing than what he experienced in 2021 after undergoing foot surgery late in spring camp.

With the help of mental skills coach Brian Cain, Jung learned in 2021 that his mind needed a distraction during the lengthy rehab process in Arizona. The rehab itself didn't take much time out of his day, so he occupied himself with the Star Wars movies and spinoffs.

Last year it was the Marvel Avengers movies and shows, and every Harry Potter movie.

He also took a few cooking courses.

The Rangers did their part. Mental performance coordinator Hannah Huesman checked in throughout spring training and after big-league camp ended, and the club tried to keep Jung's mind sharp by giving him game situations to work through.

There was some baseball. Jung would watch extended spring training games, which didn't really help him feel any better about his circumstances. In 2021, he requested virtual reality equipment from the Rangers so that he could track pitches.

Once he was cleared for the next step in the rehab process, he dived right in and searched for any way he could make himself better. His surgically repaired left shoulder, for instance, has never been stronger thanks to the work he did last spring and summer.

Jung gained strength all around and came out of the rehab process in terrific shape, hitting balls farther than ever.

Rangers vice president Ross Fenstermaker, who oversees player development, had never seen a prospect attack rehab like Jung did.

"I think it's just an insatiable desire to maximize every minute of his rehab to come back a better version," Fenstermaker said.

Jung grinded through the rehab process and returned to game action a month sooner than the initial prognosis, which put his MLB debut a possibility, and he jumped out to a hot start at Triple A Round Rock.

The media, and Jung, thought a call-up was imminent in August. But the Rangers waited and waited some more, and Jung became less selective at the plate as he tried to keep up his early pace.

Once he was promoted for his debut, he couldn't stop pressing.

So, he spent the offseason working on his approach and his swing, which was altered by the repairs to the labrum in his shoulder and that newfound strength. He felt he had found the right swing path as he headed to spring training, where he had no competition to be the starter at third.

But that didn't mean he didn't want to make an impression during Cactus League play.

"I was coming to camp wanting to leave no doubt and kind of solidify that spot," Jung said. "I felt like that coming in, they probably penciled it in and I wanted to just make sure that it was in permanent marker basically."

Perhaps the biggest assist he received in locking down the position was an early-camp conversation he had with manager Bruce Bochy. The veteran manager, who won three World Series with the San Francisco Giants in 2010, 2012 and 2014, told Jung that his focus should be on playing steady defense.

"Hitting, you're going to have your ups and downs, and you understand that, especially with a young player," Bochy said. "Hopefully, that even helped him relax that 'I don't need to hit to be on this club.' You'll be out there as long as that defense shows up on a consistent basis."

It did help him relax, Jung said. He also knows that he will be in the lineup if he goes 0 for 4 or finds himself in the kind of slump he was in last month.

The Rangers' nice start to the 2023 season has also taken pressure off Jung. They spent much of the first two months in first place in the AL West, and the Rangers had one of the most potent offenses in baseball.

The Rangers found their success without shortstop Corey Seager for much of April and May. He returned from a strained left hamstring May 17, and in his absence, Jung was one of several players who picked up the slack along with García, Marcus Semien, Jonah Heim and Ezequiel Duran.

"Oh, that makes everything way better," Jung said.

Jung is showing his teammates that he's a better player than he was last season. They have been impressed by how he has carried himself and how he is ready play every day. Not only that, he's performing.

It's an impressive package for a player who has never had more than 304 at-bats in a season.

"Experience is everything in this league, so the more he plays at this level the better he's going to be," Semien said. "He was drafted as high as he was for a reason. I'm excited to see his growth and hope I have the opportunity to play with him for many, many years."

If Jung is bothered by the high expectations, he isn't showing it.

"I feel like nothing gets to him," Semien said. "We're all just playing baseball, and he understands that. He's very mature for the amount of service time he has. That combination will take him a long way."

Jung has proven to be a tireless worker who wants to play every day. He wants to perform, even though he knows that he can't go 4 for 4 every game. He admitted that he sets the bar a little high for himself, and Young said that the Rangers have had to help him manage his expectations and not beat himself up when things aren't going well.

Jung is never satisfied.

"It's a great thing, but it can also be a crippling thing," he said. "I get too obsessed with being perfect, which is probably one of my downfalls sometimes."

The Rangers believed Jung would rebound from his shaky debut. Between injuries, they saw a player who was coachable and determined to be great. He added pull-side power after showing most of his pop to right-center field at Texas Tech.

And, boy, did he hit in the minors. He batted .311 with 30 home runs and a .919 OPS in only 602 at-bats.

"You can see some of the growth he's made at the plate with the approach," Young said. "He had a great spring. Guys normally don't deviate too far from the profile they are in the minor leagues. They may change a little bit once they get to the big leagues. We had a pretty good idea of who the player is, what he's been historically and what he's capable of."

That's why the Rangers didn't spend on a third baseman the past two offseasons. They were convinced that Jung was their third baseman.

He hasn't disappointed. ■

FINDING HIS STRIDE

Leody Taveras Looks Like Rangers' Center Fielder of the Future
May 21, 2023

Major-league baseball continues to discover how the COVID pandemic disrupted business as usual, aside from the shortening of the 2020 season and the cancelation of the minor-league season.

Disagreement between players and owners on how many games to play and when to start further sowed distrust between the two sides, and that helped fuel the lockout that shortened spring training and delayed the 2022 season.

Closing down the minor leagues in 2020 led to the alternate camp site where a small group of players served as the reserve pool in case of injuries or a lack of performance. Teams also used the alternate camp as a development ground for top prospects.

Players who otherwise would have never sniffed the big leagues ended up making their MLB debuts. What seemed like a blessing at the time has been a curse for some.

Four players who debuted that year with the Rangers can attest to that.

Two of them, Anderson Tejeda and Sherten Apostel, are no longer in the organization. Tejeda is out of baseball, while Apostel is playing in Japan.

Sam Huff is back at Triple A Round Rock and appears to have a future with the Rangers, but he will be out of options after this season because he debuted in 2020.

The other is Leody Taveras, who agrees that he shouldn't have been in the majors in 2020. He probably shouldn't have been on the Opening Day roster in 2021 and wasn't in 2022.

But things finally appear to be clicking for Taveras in his age 24 season. Yes, he's still only 24, but he now has the seasoning of someone a few years older, and it's showing on the field.

He hasn't nailed it down yet, but he is starting to look like the Rangers' everyday center fielder going forward.

"Right now, this is the result of what I had to go through and what I learned," Taveras said. "I feel good right now. That's the good thing. I'm trying to be consistent every day."

Through May 21, Taveras was batting .288 with one home run, 14 RBIs and a .355 on-base percentage after shaking off some rust from missing three weeks of spring training and opening the regular season season in the injured list.

He was batting .105 on April 19 but is batting .326 since, and that includes a 4-for-20 mini-slump the past six games despite several hard hit balls this weekend that went for outs.

His defense is another asset in the roomy center field at Globe Life Field, and he also has game-changing speed.

After multiple false starts to his major-league career, Leody Taveras found confidence in 2023 as the Rangers' everyday center fielder.

Taveras' teammates have known that he had the skills to be productive big-league player.

"He's playing really well," right fielder Adolis García said. "He has all the talent. For me, he's a five-tool player. You see the talent that he has. He's working so hard, you have to see it come around."

Taveras debuted in August of 2020 after the Rangers decided to enter a rebuild. He had played only a handful of games above High A, whereas Huff, Apostel and Tejeda had never played above A ball.

They came from the alternate site when the need arose.

Taveras held his own, or at least did enough things right for the Rangers to pencil him into center field for 2021. He didn't have a good spring, and he opened the season 4 for 46 (.087) in April before a quick demotion to Round Rock.

He appeared to strike on something at Triple A, hitting 17 homers in 302 at-bats and earning a promotion to finish out the season. But he was only marginally better, batting just .188.

No Rangers player was as negatively impacted by the lockout as Taveras, who didn't have an opportunity to work with new hitting coaches Donnie Ecker and Tim Hyers. By the time spring training started, Taveras didn't have enough time to implement the swing changes they wanted to make.

But Taveras bought in to what they were selling and took it with him to Triple A, where he was one of the best players in the minors the first month of the season. He played 99 games for Round Rock before the Rangers promoted him.

He said it was the last time he would be in the minors, and his .261 average and 18 steals convinced the Rangers to give him another chance this season.

The key to his nice start to the season has been keeping things simple.

"I made it easier and just don't think too much," Taveras said. "I trust my practice and my swing."

The switch-hitter is doing well from both sides, too. He's hitting balls harder more regularly after making some early-season adjustments in the lower half of his swing.

He has only one home run in his first 111 at-bats, but that doesn't worry him because he believes the power will show up.

Manager Bruce Bochy, who inherited Taveras when he took over for interim manager Tony Beasley, said that Taveras has lived up to the scouting report the Rangers gave him.

"I think the hitting guys have done a good job," Bochy said. "This guy's got such a high ceiling. The bat speed from both side, just a gifted athlete, I think he can be an impact-type player."

The Rangers' winning ways have also helped Taveras settle in. For the first time in his career, he has been a regular contributor to the success.

His confidence is high. He's feeling less pressure. He's taking his experiences since the COVID season and putting them to good use.

It's been a long time coming, and he doesn't have it nailed down yet, but Taveras is starting to look like the Rangers' everyday center fielder going forward.

"I knew this team in spring training that we had something," he said. "We're playing so good, and we can keep going. It's a good feeling." ∎

Leody Taveras chases a fly ball during a regular-season game against the Chicago White Sox.

IMMEDIATE IMPACT

All the History Adolis García Made with His Power Surge in Rangers' Win
April 22, 2023

The perfect game is considered by many to be the most special baseball feat, but here's a fun fact: There have been fewer four-homer games, 18, in MLB history than perfect games, 23.

Adolis García had two cracks at No. 19 on Saturday night against the Oakland Athletics, including one against a position player.

"We were all pulling for him," manager Bruce Bochy said.

Alas, García had to settle for three home runs, two doubles, eight RBIs, going 5 for 5 and collecting 16 total bases as the Rangers routed the A's 18-3.

The home runs were all three-run shots and all hit with two outs, in the first, third and fifth innings. His doubles came in the seventh and the ninth. He was also hit by a pitch in the second inning.

"It was incredible," García said. "I didn't expect something like that to happen."

He did make a lot of history.

- García became only the third player in the modern era (since 1901) with at least 16 total bases, three homers, eight RBIs and five runs in one game. The others were Anthony Rendon in 2017 for Washington and Gil Hodges in 1950 for Brooklyn.

- He became the first player in American League history with a three-homer, two-double game, and his performance was the 14th instance in MLB history of a player with five extra-base hits in a game.

- It was the 19th game in Rangers history when a player record at least three home runs. The last was Ronald Guzman in 2018 at Yankee Stadium.

- Josh Hamilton hit four home runs and a double in a 2012 game at Baltimore and owns the club record for total bases in a game with 18. García is second.

- García tied the club record for runs in a game, the first time that had happened since Ian Kinsler's 6-for-6 cycle game in 2009, and matched Hamilton's club record for extra-base hits in a game.

- The eight RBIs are tied for second in club history. The club record is nine by Ivan Rodriguez in 1999 at Seattle.

- The three-homer game was the first in Globe Life Field history.

Adolis García celebrates in the dugout after hitting his third home run of the night against the Oakland Athletics. The slugger proved to be one of the Rangers' most dynamic players throughout the 2023 season.

"It's fun to watch great athletes when they're locked in have a great night," Bochy said.

García batted in seventh against James Kapriellian and ripped a double into the gap in right-center field for his seventh and eight RBIs. The eight RBIs vaulted García into the MLB lead for RBIs with 28.

The ball was hit 107.5 mph, which wasn't as hard as the first two homers (109.1 and 108.1) but was harder than the third (99.1).

He batted again in the ninth against second baseman Jace Peterson, who was just lobbing the ball to the plate. Travis Jankowski reached with one out, which meant that reliever Josh Sborz could do anything but hit into a double play for García to have one last chance.

"He had orders not to swing the bat," said Bochy, who was also concerned about Sborz injuring himself on a swing. Sborz was batting because Bochy had inserted designated hitter Brad Miller at first base and lost the DH spot in the lineup.

The bat never left Sborz's shoulder, which set the stage for García.

He ended up with a double over third base that rolled into the left-field corner.

"It's difficult," García said. "My timing was off. I wanted to hit a homer in that last at-bat." ■

Adolis García is showered with sports drink after his powerhouse evening at the plate.

STAR-STUDDED

Voters Elect Four Texas Rangers as All-Star Starters
June 29, 2023

Baseball fans have spoken, and they seem to like the Texas Rangers.

Catcher Jonah Heim, second baseman Marcus Semien, third baseman Josh Jung and shortstop Corey Seager were elected as starters for the American League team at the 93rd All-Star Game, to take place July 11 in Seattle.

Heim and Jung are first-time All-Stars, and they join Seager as first-time All-Star starters. Seager is a four-time All-Star, and Semien has been voted a starter in both of his appearances.

Adolis García finished fifth in the outfield race.

All five advanced to Phase 2 of the voting. Semien, Jung and Seager enjoyed large leads all week, while Heim's race with Orioles catcher Adley Rutschman went down to the wire.

The Rangers hadn't had an All-Star starter since 2012. Now, they have four.

"The fans acknowledged us this year. I guess we're doing something," Semien said. "The starters are voted by the fans, and the team did a good job marketing us."

All four starters did a good job marketing themselves with their play.

Semien leads baseball in runs scored and is second in the AL in hits. Jung was selected as the AL Rookie of the Month the first two months of the season. Seager would be leading the league in batting average if he had enough at-bats to qualify.

Heim might be a surprise pick, but he has more home runs and more RBIs than Rutschman in fewer at-bats.

"It's exciting," Heim said. "I don't think it's truly set in yet. It's a tremendous honor to represent the organization like this."

Jung is only the second rookie all time to be a starter at third base, and the last was Eddie Kazak for the 1949 Cardinals.

"It's really special," Jung said. "We've pretty much got the whole infield. It's going to be fun to share it with those guys."

Seager and Semien signed with the Rangers late in 2021, just before the lockout, for a combined $500 million. Seager was selected as an All-Star replacement last season, but neither he nor Semien were thrilled with their first season.

Seager is batting .345 with a 1.020 OPS despite missing five weeks with a hamstring injury.

"Any time you can make one is really fun, whether you miss time or not," he said. "It's just really exciting." ■

Second baseman Marcus Semien was voted an All-Star Game starter for the second year in a row.

ALL-STAR MOMENTS

July 12, 2023

Five Rangers started Tuesday night for the American League All-Star team, the most for any team since the 1956 Cincinnati Reds.

In the second inning, all six of their All-Stars were on the field. That tied the all-time record for most players playing from one team playing at the same time, matching the 1939 Yankees.

The AL team didn't win, losing 3-2 as the National League snapped a nine-game losing streak, and the Rangers were a collective 0 for 9 at the plate. But Nathan Eovaldi tossed a scoreless second inning, Jonah Heim threw out a runner, and Adolis García battled the sun to make two leaping catches at the right-field wall to give the AL a chance.

Now, after a cross-country flight, a couple commercial shoots, media day, the Home Run Derby, and a long run from the outfield to home plate in pregame introductions, the six Rangers All-Stars can finally get a little rest.

The Rangers will have a workout Thursday, though the All-Stars won't be required to attend. It wouldn't be a surprise if workaholics Marcus Semien and Josh Jung showed up. Corey Seager can roll out of bed and get a hit, so he might just do that.

The season resumes Friday at Globe Life Field. That's when the heavy lifting begins for the Rangers.

Adolis García catches a fly ball hit by Sean Murphy of the Atlanta Braves in the fourth inning of the All-Star Game at T-Mobile Park in Seattle.

Josh Jung jogs out on the red carpet as he is introduced as the starting third baseman at MLB's All-Star Game. Jung became the first Rangers rookie to start an All-Star Game since the franchise moved to Texas in 1972.

Jonah Heim suits up before his start at catcher for the American League All-Star team.

5

SHORTSTOP

....

COREY SEAGER

'It's Pretty Special What You're Seeing Him Do on the Field'
July 2023

With five players who have won the American League MVP and 15 who have been named Silver Slugger Award winners, the Rangers have had no shortage of offensive highlights through the years.

Within those award-worthy seasons were piles of home runs and RBIs, and, for the most part, team wins.

The most notable providers of great moments were Ivan Rodriguez, Josh Hamilton, Juan Gonzalez, Adrian Beltre and Alex Rodriguez. But it's not an exclusive club.

All-Stars such as Michael Young, Ian Kinsler, Joey Gallo and Rafael Palmeiro chipped in. Even those with short-lived Rangers stints, like Dave Hostetler, Gabe Kapler and Bengie Molina, had big moments in franchise history.

Corey Seager is joining all of them this season.

Since coming off the injured list in mid-May, Seager has been one of the top performers in all of baseball. His at-bats have become must-see TV. It's a shock when he doesn't hit a ball harder than 100 mph. Even his outs often follow good contact.

It's not as if Seager wasn't a good player in 2022, his first with the Rangers after signing a 10-year, $325 million contract. He was an All-Star who connected for 33 home runs, an MLB record for a left-handed-hitting shortstop.

But he has been an MVP-caliber player in 2023.

Corey Seager slides into third base on a double by Evan Carter during Game 1 of the World Series.

"He missed, what, a month of the season and he's beating us in RBIs and doubles and all this stuff," third baseman Josh Jung said. "It's awesome."

Manager Bruce Bochy fielded lineups at previous stops that included Tony Gwynn, arguably baseball's best hitter the past 50 years, and Barry Bonds, baseball's all-time leader in home runs. Seager reminds Bochy of the former San Diego Padres and San Francisco Giants stars with his ability to consistently make solid contact.

"He's just got a knack for putting the barrel on the ball consistently — lefties, righties, whoever," Bochy said. "We're lucky to have him, I know that. I've seen some good hitters and have been able to manage some good hitters, but he's right up there. That's how good I think he is."

Seager drove in the 500th run on his career July 14 against Cleveland with a double hit with an exit velocity of 107.2 mph and connected in his next at-bat for his 150th career homer on a ball hit at 101.6 mph. He lined out to center field earlier in the game at 110.7 mph.

He finished the day second in baseball with an average exit velocity of 94.9 mph, behind only Yankees slugger Aaron Judge.

During a five-hit game June 10 at Tampa Bay, the softest contact Seager made was 98 mph.

In his first game after missing 31 contests because of a strained left hamstring, Seager stung two balls at 106.6 mph and 105.5 mph, the second off left-hander Mike Minter for a sacrifice fly.

That performance, and the following two months, came after only five at-bats on a rehab assignment with Double A Frisco.

"I was just in the right position," Seager said. "I wholeheartedly believe if you're in the right position, you'll swing at pitches you need to. If not, you'll be swinging at the ones you're not supposed to. And sometimes it happens in five at-bats. Sometimes you don't need any. Sometimes it takes 20. I was just fortunate enough to find it faster than I could have."

Said Bochy: "That tells you how good he is."

"He works on his craft every day, and he's found something that works," second baseman Marcus Semien said.

Seager was one of four Rangers players who were voted as starters for the All-Star Game, along with Semien, Jung and catcher Jonah Heim, and one of five total starters after right fielder Adolis Garcia filled one of the two outfield vacancies created by injuries to Judge and Mike Trout.

It was Seager's fourth All-Star selection but just his first start. The AL manager, Astros manager Dusty Baker, praised Seager.

"He's got a smooth left-handed swing, but he's trying to do something with it," Baker said. "He can scissor with his legs. I was trying to teach my guys that because he uses his legs as well as anybody in this league. I tried to teach my son that. I think it runs in his family. I bet his mama could hit."

Seager has never been one to talk about himself, good or bad, but he recognizes now how difficult it is for a player to switch teams. Seager had been with the Dodgers since 2012, when they selected him the 18th overall pick. He was the MVP of the National League Championship Series and the World Series in 2020 as Globe Life Field served as the host site during the COVID postseason.

He signed with the Rangers, along with Semien and right-hander Jon Gray, only hours before the MLB lockout started. The newcomers were unable to speak to club personnel until the lockout ended in March.

Spring training was shortened, giving Seager less time to acquaint himself with his new teammates and for them to get acquainted with him. The same went for Semien,

Corey Seager missed over a month of play at the start of the 2023 season, but he quickly returned to form as one of the Rangers' top producers.

Seager's double-play partner up the middle.

"The more double plays we turn, the better we're going to be," said Semien, who made his second All-Star appearance last month. "Any person I play with up in the middle there's going to be chemistry. You build that in spring training. We're going to play there for a long time. As time goes on, we're going to build confidence."

Seager goes about his routine at the ballpark differently than most, choosing to not take batting practice on the field. He takes groundballs with his teammates, but usually only before the first game of each series.

There was an adjustment period for some of his teammates.

"Getting used to personality and learning who they are as a person off the field, too," first baseman Nathaniel Lowe said. "Some players do that quicker than others. It's good that in Year 2 they can start to come into their own."

Seager understands that side of it, too, but everything that was new last year is old hat now.

"It's become normal," he said. "Everything's normalized. I know where everything is now. You know who everybody is. Just the feeling of not being the new guy is a lot easier.

"The whole working relationship, personal relationship stuff has been figured out. It's give-and-take on both sides. How can I help ease in my routine and how can they help ease me into my routine as well? So it's been all pretty much figured out, and it's just shut up and go to work every day now."

Winning has also helped. The Dodgers went to the postseason in each of Seager's seven seasons. He knew last season what it took to win games, but much of the rest of the club was still trying to figure that out in their initial seasons in the majors.

It is a skill that takes time, and sometimes a lot of lumps, to learn.

"There were points throughout the season where you just kind of sit there and wonder, 'What's going on? Why can't we make this better? Why isn't it better? How do we make it better to get to where it should be?" Seager said. "And I feel like we've done a good job of that."

The key to sustaining success down the stretch is not looking too far ahead. That's something veterans know but younger players like Jung and Taveras might need to be reminded of.

"Playing tonight, trying to win tonight, win the series," Seager said. "As soon as you start looking ahead, the moment gets away from you and you start slipping. It's a hard thing to do. It's very monotonous. But that's how you have success over 162 games, being monotonous. It's something we're just going to have to continue working on, talking about and being on top of."

The Rangers kept their foot on the pedal in the offseason with the free-agent signings of right-handers Jacob deGrom and Nathan Eovaldi and left-handers Martin Perez and Andrew Heaney. The team made a savvy signing after spring training started when they landed closer Will Smith on a one-year deal.

Jung has helped fill one of the holes from 2022, and Leody Taveras and Ezequiel Duran have matured into winning players.

Rangers brass, including general manager Chris Young, former president of baseball operations Jon Daniels and former manager Chris Woodward, presented Seager with their vision for the Rangers in upcoming seasons, and so far the Rangers have delivered.

"That's kind of to a tee of what I was told," he said. "They wanted to go get guys. They wanted to go get starting pitching. I guess, unfortunately, for me and Marcus, the pitching wasn't the same year. And then they talked about the minor leagues and what was coming. And it's been spot on."

The players still had to do their part, and much of the change was on the mental side. The Rangers' last postseason appearance was in 2016, when they won a franchise-record 96 games but were swept by Toronto in the division series.

That was also the Rangers' last winning campaign. Only one team was worse than them in 2020 and just two were worse in 2021 as they lost 102 times. The 2022 team went 68-94, which was the seventh-worst record in baseball.

When the 2023 Rangers show up, they expect to win every game.

"When you can go out there and compete every game and expect to win, that's a pretty special thing," Seager said. "I think that's kind of what we're building here and trying to get people to understand and know that it's possible. When you've lost that much, you kind of expect things to go bad. You've got to change the thought process and the narrative."

Bochy is making a difference with that in his first season.

He came to the Rangers after a three-year hiatus, but also with three World Series rings with the Giants and more than 2,000 career victories. His first World Series title came against the Rangers in 2010.

Seager considers Woodward instrumental in his development, especially defensively, and he was part of the reason Seager signed with the Rangers. He doesn't have a bad word to say about the Rangers' manager from 2019 until August 2022.

But Bochy's pedigree speaks for itself.

"Their personalities are definitely different," Seager said. "I don't want to say respect because respect is the wrong word. But Bochy has been a proven winner. And when you have that reputation, just that standard of being here this long, being in every situation, I feel like you get accepted better.

"He's done an incredible job. He's been welcoming. He's been humorous. He's connected with people. He's been awesome."

So has Seager, who said he steps into the batter's box looking for a fastball and then adjusts to off-speed pitches. He's not afraid to go after the first pitch, either.

"Hit it hard and forward," he said.

Lowe has hit third most of the year, one spot behind Seager, so he has had as good of a view as anyone else for Seager's at-bats. With the advent of the pitch clock, Seager gets in the box and stays there. He hadn't used a timeout during the Rangers' first 94 games and had no plans to use one.

"You can tell when he's ready," Lowe said. "If he's going to take 40 at-bats in a well, there's probably 35 of them where I'm just standing back and thinking, 'OK, this is going in the seats or in the gap.' He looks like he's always ready."

This season, his second with the Rangers, Seager looks like an MVP.

"It's pretty special what you're seeing him do on the field," Heim said. ■

RIGHTING THE SHIP

A Tumultuous Week in 2022 Started Rangers on Winning Path
August 13, 2023

Giants fans sure love them some Bruce Bochy; their tributes and ovations for the visiting Rangers manager made that clear. And why wouldn't they? Bochy is best remembered in baseball circles as the Giants manager who in 2010 led them to their first World Series title since moving to San Francisco. He tacked on two more in 2012 and 2014.

When he retired in 2019 after 13 seasons, he left with the second-most victories in franchise history (1,052). Nobody is catching John McGraw.

At 68, Bochy probably doesn't have 13 seasons with the Rangers in him. He signed a three-year deal in October 2022 after being wooed off the couch and back to the bench by general manager Chris Young.

Bochy replaced interim manager Tony Beasley, who finished the season after Chris Woodward was fired.

Woodward was dismissed a year ago with the Rangers 51-63.

Not all of what ailed the Rangers during Woodward's reign from 2019 to 2022 was his fault. Very little of it was. Oh, by the way, he wasn't the only key decision-maker fired that week.

Not all of what is unfolding in Bochy's first season, including the Rangers becoming the fastest team in franchise history to reach 70 wins (117 games), is his doing.

Much of it is, though.

THE OTHER CHANGE

During the news conference announcing Woodward's ouster, president of baseball operations Jon Daniels admitted that the Rangers hadn't built a championship-caliber roster, but they expected to be better than they were.

Daniels was fired two days later, leaving Young in charge of the franchise.

Daniels was more culpable for the Rangers' losing ways than Woodward, but it's always important to remember that even Daniels had a boss who set the budget and signed off on his decisions.

Young deserves credit for the Rangers' success this season, but he doesn't take all of it. He knows that Daniels' fingerprints, and those of the personnel he hired and Young inherited, are all over this Rangers team.

Adolis García, Nate Lowe, Josh Jung, Leody Taveras, Brock Burke and Dane Dunning all came to the organization before Young, and Jonah Heim and Josh Sborz came while Young was still adjusting to being a GM under Daniels. Those are victories for pro scouts and amateur scouts hired by Daniels.

Young and Daniels tag-teamed on the 2021 trade of Joey Gallo for four prospects, including Ezequiel Duran and Josh Smith, and the free-agent signings of Corey Seager, Marcus Semien and Jon Gray.

The Rangers did spend lavishly in the offseason on

Bruce Bochy acknowledges San Francisco Giants fans as he receives a standing ovation at Oracle Park before a regular-season series against his former team.

pitching, guided by Young. Seager and Semien are living up to their contracts. Younger players are producing after struggling the past two seasons as they learned the ropes under Woodward.

But the new manager brings unparalleled experience and respect to the Rangers' dugout.

EXHIBIT A

Bochy's managing in the Rangers' 70th win, a 9-3 victory in San Francisco, was some of his best in the 2023 season.

Starting pitcher Andrew Heaney wasn't throwing enough strikes. He allowed a run in the first, then loaded the bases with no outs in the second. He was fortunate to come back from behind in the count to strike out Mark Mathias, but Bochy had seen enough.

Heaney was removed after only four outs and 40 pitches. Bochy said afterward that Heaney had been dealing with an illness and didn't throw a bullpen between starts. He wasn't in his best form, so Bochy went and got him, even though it would force the bullpen to work 7 2/3 innings.

It worked like a charm. Grant Anderson came in and got a double play to end the inning. Chris Stratton cleaned up an Anderson mess a few innings later and provided three scoreless innings.

The offense figured out Alex Cobb and wore him down. They did the same to reliever Alex Wood and kept piling on.

Bochy and Mike Maddux, who was lured by Bochy to return to the Rangers rather than retiring as a pitching coach, had a plan to protect Heaney if necessary and still win a ballgame. They followed through with it.

Would Woodward have done the same thing? Maybe. Woodward, whose option for 2023 had been picked up in spring training, never had an opportunity to show if he was a good tactical manager, because he was seemingly always trying to develop players during the Rangers' rebuild.

With three previous World Series wins and over 2,000 career managerial wins, Bruce Bochy brings unparalleled experience to the Texas Rangers.

Through no fault of his own, he didn't have the instant credibility Bochy has, nor had he been through the same number of situations. Nothing surprises Bochy or catches him off guard.

The scenario with Heaney, which in the moment seemed risky, wasn't anything Bochy didn't know how to handle. The rest of the team rolled with it.

A YEAR LATER

Rangers players quickly adapted to Bochy, who talked to them in spring training about togetherness and tackling the fundamentals. The Rangers are playing cleaner defense, and they haven't folded when a key player or two has gone on the injured list.

Their 70th win of the season was also their fifth straight series win. Not bad for a team that won only 60 and 68 games the past two seasons and was a combined 84 games below .500 the past three seasons.

The Bochy hire, orchestrated solely by Young (a former player of his) is not the only reason the Rangers are winning. But he was the Rangers' key offseason acquisition — no offense to Maddux, Heaney, Nathan Eovaldi, Jacob deGrom or Will Smith (a former reliever under Bochy).

Now, the Rangers are on a winning path. ■

Rangers GM Chris Young introduces Bruce Bochy as the Rangers' new manager in October 2022. Young previously played under Bochy when the two were with the San Diego Padres.

31
PITCHER

MAX SCHERZER

Rangers' Veteran Acquisition is Looking Out for Future Generations
September 2023

A start day for Max Scherzer is described by his teammates as intense from the moment he steps in the Rangers clubhouse.

He's not unapproachable, though some around the team are so apprehensive they aren't even sure if they should tell him hello. He will talk about baseball stuff, teammates say, but doesn't have time for any other BS as he gets ready to attack the lineup that will soon be in front of him.

Once he pops out from the dugout, the intensity meter is turned even higher. He doesn't give in, even when he's trying to navigate a tough spot. When an inning his over, he goes to the dugout and discusses how to approach the next set of hitters he'll be facing.

He already knows but abides by legendary college basketball coach John Wooden's famous saying: A failure to prepare is preparing to fail.

"You understand what makes him good," manager Bruce Bochy said. "I'm not just talking about just the day he pitches. It's his bullpen. He's unwavering with his conditioning and being ready for that start."

The Rangers acquired the three-time Cy Young winner July 31 from the Mets for minor-league shortstop Luisangel Acuña. Scherzer exercised the player option he had for 2024, and the Mets sent $36 million to help the Rangers cover the tab.

Max Scherzer's trade to the Rangers reunited him with pitching coach Mike Maddux, who was there for both of Scherzer's Cy Young award-winning seasons with the Washington Nationals.

The deal might end up being a bargain if the 39-year-old helps push the Rangers to the postseason this season or next. That's why general manager Chris Young made the deal, and all Scherzer wants as he starts to run out of seasons is another World Series ring.

That pursuit is why he's still battling, but he's been battling ever since the Arizona Diamondbacks drafted him in 2006 and promptly told him that he wasn't healthy and wasn't built to be a major-league starting pitcher.

For those who wonder how Scherzer can still be so focused and so driven, those traits might have taken root during his post-draft experience.

"I came into the game in a fight," Scherzer said. "I hated it. But at the end of day, you had to do it. You have to defend yourself. You have to learn more about yourself as a person going through that to withstand people trying to tear you down and say things that you're not and you have to believe that you are."

The Diamondbacks' approach seems odd for the 11th overall pick, and Scherzer thought so, too. He didn't get the red-carpet treatment that first-rounders usually receive.

It was so bad that Scherzer's first professional appearance was in independent ball for the Fort Worth Cats in 2007. He made only three starts, posting a scant 0.56 ERA and striking out 25 overmatched hitters in 16 innings.

Though he made his major-league debut only two years after he was drafted, Scherzer was a hardened rookie. He was a good rookie, with stuff that was sometimes better than his control of it.

He was 9-15 in parts of two seasons with Arizona, but he had a 3.52 ERA and 240 strikeouts in 226 1/3 innings. He walked 84, which wasn't particularly wild but wasn't as pinpoint as his control has become.

He went 1-2 with a 2.70 ERA in three 2009 starts against the Giants, who were managed by Bochy and a year away from their first World Series title as they beat the Rangers in five games.

"We knew what great stuff he had," Bochy said. "He homed in some of the wildness that you're going to have for a young guy. But it was really good stuff."

The Diamondbacks didn't see Scherzer's future coming. They traded him after the 2009 season to Detroit in a headline-grabbing three-team deal that included the Yankees getting Curtis Granderson from the Tigers. Arizona received Edwin Jackson.

Advantage, Tigers.

They added Scherzer to a rotation that included Justin Verlander and Rick Porcello to become a force in the American League. It helped that they also had two-time MVP Miguel Cabrera.

Scherzer's first taste of the postseason was in 2011, when he pitched twice against the Rangers in 2011 American League Championship Series. He posted a quality start in Game 2 but took a no-decision in a game decided in the 11th inning by Nelson Cruz's walk-off grand slam off the left-field foul pole.

The Rangers jumped on Scherzer in Game 6, which ended up being the clincher. He took a 2-0 lead into the third inning but allowed six runs while recording only one out. The Rangers scored nine times in the third, en route to a 15-5 victory and their second straight appearance in the World Series.

Scherzer helped the Tigers go to the World Series the next year, where they were swept in four games by Bochy's Giants. Scherzer guided the Tigers to the ALCS in 2013, where they lost to the Red Sox.

After the season, Scherzer was awarded his first Cy Young for a season in which he went 21-3 with a 2.90 ERA and 240 strikeouts in 214 1/3 innings. The vote wasn't

Max Scherzer looks on before a regular-season game between the Texas Rangers and the Los Angeles Angels of Anaheim.

close as he received 28 of the 30 first-place tallies to top Rangers ace Yu Darvish.

Free agency beckoned after a solid 2014 (18-5, 3.15 ERA), and the Washington Nationals came calling with a seven-year, $210 million contract. As big as the deal was, the Nationals got their money's worth.

Scherzer went 92-47 with a 2.80 ERA in 189 starts, won two Cy Young awards and helped the Nationals to a World Series triumph over the Astros in 2019. He firmly established himself as one of the game's elite pitchers.

His pitching coach for both Cy Young seasons was Mike Maddux, who landed with the Nationals after his exit from the Rangers following the 2015 season. Maddux returned to the Rangers this season, and his presence on the coaching staff helped Scherzer make a smooth transition after the Rangers acquired him.

Though six seasons have passed, Maddux said that Scherzer still has the same mechanics and the same focus and intensity that he had when guiding the 2016 and 2017 Nationals to back-to-back National League East crowns.

Maddux remembers the same highlights as everyone else, including a 20-strikeout game, but the things no one else sees stood out the most to Maddux. Scherzer was durable, as his multiple 200-inning seasons suggest, but he knew his body and what it would take to get there.

"There was a game in Miami, where he came up hit a three-run homer and took himself out of the game, didn't even go out and warm up the next inning because he knew that he was jeopardizing himself and the team if he went out there and tried to pitch through what he was dealing with," Maddux said.

"His awareness to listen to his body is one reason he's had the longevity. That stands out to me, the way he understands his body and his limits. But then there's other times when he gets rolling, he's going to go until he's got 27 outs or is out of bullets."

Maddux echoed what Rangers teammates have seen of Scherzer during a game. He talks. He wants information about what Maddux and the catchers might have seen the previous inning and how to go about the next one.

"He's very vocal," Maddux said. "As far as communication during the game, it's nonstop."

Maddux has worked with All-Stars and another Cy Young winner, C.C. Sabathia, during his lengthy coaching career with the Brewers, the Rangers, the Nationals and the Cardinals. His brother is in the Hall of Fame.

Scherzer's work ethic is at the upper echelon of those Maddux has coached or seen from across the field.

"Oh man, he's in the top 5 percent," Maddux said. "The guys that hang around a long time, it's not by accident. Work ethic is part of their fabric, and that's why they're able to hang around, and they understand that. The older you get, the harder you have to work and the more rest you need. So figure that out."

Along the way, Scherzer has also taken on an active role with the Major League Baseball Players Association. Baseball has been good to Scherzer, very good, and he wants it to be a better place for the next generation of players.

He said he was fascinated with how the union came to be, beginning with Curt Flood's landmark case in which he challenged the reserve clause that bound a player to a team for his entire career, barring a trade.

Though the U.S. Supreme Court ruled against Flood, the wheels were set in motion for free agency that was ushered in in 1976 when an arbitrator ruled that Andy Messersmith and Dave McNally, who were playing without a contract, were free agents.

Flood ruined his career when he refused a trade from the Cardinals to the Phillies and then sued baseball. But he wanted things to be better for future generations, and his case helped accomplish that.

Scherzer was at the forefront during the labor strife that resulted in a lockout on Dec. 1, 2021, that stretched into March. Scherzer was on the MLBPA's executive subcommittee along with Rangers second baseman Marcus Semien.

The players feel like they negotiated some, but not all, of the things they wanted.

"He definitely was a strong reason we made some progress," Semien said. "His strengths, his leadership, it seems like anything he's doing, he's giving it 100 percent. His teammates gravitate toward him whether it's playing baseball or union stuff. His personality makes him somebody to follow."

Scherzer, now in his 16th season, doesn't shy away from cameras and notepads. His press conferences are downright fun, and interviews at his locker might turn into a 20-minute talk.

He said that he won't be pushing Semien to be the Rangers' union representative, but he is surely going to be a sounding board for Semien if a critical issue arises.

"I'm retired from the union," he said. "I put my time. I've got too many kids. I don't have time anymore. I can't do the phone calls anymore. I'm glad I did it. I served my time. I gave everything I had for those basically five years. But I just don't have the time to be on the front lines anymore."

But he's proud of the work he did. He realizes that baseball has made him and his family financially secure for generations, and he credits the players who came before him. He wants the same to happen for the future players.

"I feel like it's part of my duty to make sure that the next generation, they are able to realize their contracts and, more importantly, make sure that the game is right, that the structure of the game compensates the players in a correct manner," he said.

His focus now is on the task at hand — getting the Rangers to the postseason. He did his part immediately after the trade, leading the Rangers to victories in his first three starts. He wasn't the only new addition to the rotation, as the Rangers added left-hander Jordan Montgomery from the Cardinals in a deal that also included reliever Chris Stratton.

Scherzer said he came to the Rangers knowing that they were a good team. Their first-place record and six All-Stars were indicators of that. Being around the club, though, has him convinced that the Rangers can win in October.

He knew all about Semien and Corey Seager, his one-time teammate with the Dodgers. The supporting cast, though, is mostly new to him, and they give the Rangers a chance to win it all as much as the guys with the big contracts.

"I've played with Corey, I know how great he is and he's having a great year," Scherzer said. "But it's guys like [Leody Taveras], it's guys like Ezekiel Durán, Jonah [Heim], [Mitch] Garver and all these other guys that you might write about as much that make this team really special and what they're able to do. That's what's been great to come over here and get with those guys and just feel the vibe of the clubhouse and just try to add to it."

Scherzer has done that with talent, but also the fight, intensity and preparedness he's had since he had to battle his way into professional baseball.

"When you look at elite players and see what makes them great and why they played so long ... that focus that he has," Bochy said. "In our game you've got to have talent, but you've got to have that mental toughness. I think that's what separates the good ones and the great ones.

"It's how he prepares, how he hits that mound, that competitive spirit he has, too. He's all-in on finding a way to win a ballgame." ∎

'THIS IS ELECTRIC'

Evan Carter Provides Late-Season Boost for Rangers' Playoff Chase
September 24, 2023

Tracking the careers of the 23,086 players who debuted in the majors before him tells us that Evan Carter isn't always going to be this good.

He's up to a whopping 40 career at-bats, theoretically on his way to 7,000 or 8,000. He's only 21 after all.

Carter is a young 21, too, having gained legal drinking status Aug. 29.

At some point over the next 7,960 at-bats, he's going to chase a pitch out of the strike zone or make some kind of other mistake. His heart rate will tick up. He might even get so flustered that he curses.

He has played in 14 major-league games, all which have come in the thick of a pennant chase, and he's reached in every one of them. The Rangers are 9-5 when he's been in the lineup.

Carter has become indispensable.

"It's pretty special," shortstop Corey Seager said.

Carter entered Sunday batting .325 with a .440 on-base percentage, a .675 slugging percentage, three home runs, nine walks and a 199 OPS+. His on-base streak is a club record for a rookie to start his career.

Carter has the best strike-zone judgment on the team, and he might be the Rangers' fastest player. He's a future leadoff man who posted a .410 on-base percentage in 1,134 minor-league plate appearances, and he has enough power to give his team a 1-0 lead.

So does second baseman Marcus Semien, who has a club-record nine leadoff homers this season along with a league-best 115 runs. He's second in hits with 176 and fourth in doubles with 38, tied with first baseman Nate Lowe.

By batting ninth, Carter acts as a leadoff man ahead of Semien and Seager.

Carter displayed his power and eye in the recent series opener against the Mariners, swatting a three-run homer in the second inning and drawing a walk to jump-start a four-run fifth.

Many young players in the majors for the first time have tried to do too much, whether they realize it or not. Carter is doing as much or as little as game situations call for.

The biggest game he'd played in previous to the Rangers' playoff chase? The 2022 Texas League championship series with Double A Frisco.

"Oh, my gosh," Carter said. "This is electric. You get out there and you can't hear yourself think sometimes."

The magnitude of the situation isn't lost on him.

"I know how important this is, and I know how close everything is," he said. "But at the same time, I play best when I'm relaxed. I'm just trying to treat each game like it's just another game. Oh, my gosh, it's easier said than done, but that's what I try to do."

Manager Bruce Bochy has managed his share of ballyhooed prospects. Catcher Buster Posey came to the Giants seemingly as a savior, was the 2012 MVP and won three World Series rings. So far Carter's maturity rates highly among Bochy's best.

Evan Carter heads to bat during his major-league debut against the Oakland Athletics in September.

Carter is the Rangers' top prospect and No. 8 in baseball.

"He just has a quiet confidence about him. Very calm," Bochy said. "He plays the game. He slows it down. He's taking close pitches, does a good job in the outfield, so he's just been a shot in the arm for us."

Carter, it appears, is never going back to the minor leagues. The Rangers have a need next season for an affordable everyday left fielder, where Carter said he is happy to play despite being a center fielder. Leody Taveras, in the midst of a very good season, is the center fielder but said he is fine playing left field.

Like everyone else on the team, Taveras has been impressed by Carter.

"He's an unbelievable guy," Taveras said. "He can do everything. It's a privilege to play with him."

Taveras was a few weeks shy of turning 22 when he made his MLB debut during the 2020 COVID season but has spent time the past two seasons in the minor leagues.

This season marks his first MLB campaign without being on option to the minors (he opened the season in the minors on a rehab assignment). His WAR, according to Baseball-Reference, is 2.4

"I'm seeing good results," said Taveras, whose defense Saturday night was praised by Bochy. "I'm helping the team. That's most important. There's nothing more I can ask for."

Depending on how the Rangers allocate their budget in the off-season, a bat might not be a priority with the season Taveras has had and with what Carter has shown.

Carter, who has become indispensable, isn't going anywhere.

"I've been having a really good time," he said. "The goal would be to remain up here for the rest of your career, to be up here and help the team win. You never know what's going to happen, but I'm going to do everything I can to help the team win." ∎

Originally selected by the Rangers in the second round of the 2020 draft, Evan Carter quickly became a breakout star following his late-season promotion to the major-league squad.

LEAGUE PLAYOFFS

AMERICAN LEAGUE WILD CARD SERIES GAME 1
October 3, 2023 · St. Petersburg, Florida
Rangers 4, Rays 0

DOING THE LITTLE THINGS

Montgomery Dazzles On and Off the Mound in Game 1 Win

Jose Siri isn't known for his bunting prowess, and it showed when he tried to lay one down in the second inning.

The Tampa Bay outfielder popped it up, pushing it toward the first-base line, but it caught the Rangers by surprise and appeared as if it was going to fall for a hit that would load the bases for the Rays.

Jordan Montgomery isn't known for his fielding prowess. But the Rangers left-hander knew where first baseman Nathaniel Lowe was positioned, and he morphed into a Gold Glover.

Montgomery's full-length diving catch just before the bunt hit the turf was arguably the biggest play in the Rangers' 4-0 Game 1 victory to open the American League best-of-3 wild-card round.

"I knew Nate was playing back, so it was my ball," he said. "I saw it high enough in the air, kind of made two quick steps at it, and then kind of just blacked out and went for it."

The play helped Montgomery scatter six hits in seven innings, and Corey Seager, Leody Taveras and Evan Carter each collected two hits as the Rangers moved one win away from advancing to the division series this weekend at Baltimore.

Montgomery was aching some after his catch, and athletic trainer Matt Lucero, among others, went to the mound to check on him. Montgomery said that he landed on his right shoulder and hip and also scraped up his pitching hand some.

Lowe said that he was thinking about diving for the ball until he saw Montgomery quickly, relatively, get off the mound. Lowe and manager Bruce Bochy agreed that the play, as much as anything else in seven innings, showed how much Montgomery wants to win.

"It wasn't a soft landing, was it?" Bochy said. "We were in a tight situation there, so a big play at that point in the game, and it just shows you how competitive he is to go out there and dive for that ball."

Carter made a diving catch to end the first inning, and aside from his bobble in left field in the sixth inning, the Rangers played flawless defense. They also took six walks, allowed only one, and took advantage of four Rays errors.

Jordan Montgomery pitched seven scoreless innings in the Wild Card series opener, while also showing off some defensive prowess.

At this time of the year, when every out matters and nearly every game is tight, those things make the biggest difference.

"The little things matter," Seager said. "Runs are hard to come by, and you're trying to prevent them as much as possible. Being sharp on defense is a big thing."

When Carter wasn't collecting his two hits, both doubles, he was drawing walks. He walked in the second inning, doubled in the fourth, walked and scored a key run in the sixth, and doubled to start the eighth.

The long run Carter scored in the sixth was the first of two to score on a Seager single to center field that Siri misplayed. Siri compounded his bobble by throwing the ball into the Rangers' dugout in an attempt to get Marcus Semien at third. Instead, Semien scored to make it 4-0.

After Montgomery pitched around an Isaac Parades single and the Carter error with two outs in the sixth, he pitched around a one-out single in the seventh. After he struck out pinch-hitter Junior Caminero to end the inning, Montgomery let out a scream that could be heard over the moans of a sparse Tropicana Field crowd (19,407).

"Playoff baseball gets everybody a little extra excited," said catcher Jonah Heim, who pumped his fist as he headed to the dugout. "When you see emotion out of him, something good happened. He made a good pitch when he needed to. Seven shutout in a wild-card game on the road, you can do whatever you want."

The victory doesn't allow the Rangers to take their foot off the gas. If anything, they know they left some runs on the bases, stranding 13 runners.

"Winning Game 1 is huge," Semien said. ■

Rangers first baseman Nathaniel Lowe looks on as his brother, Rays outfielder Josh Lowe, adjusts his gear.

AMERICAN LEAGUE WILD CARD SERIES GAME 2
October 4, 2023 · St. Petersburg, Florida
Rangers 7, Rays 1

SWEEP!

Eovaldi, Carter Knock Out Rays as Rangers Advance

Left on the side of the baseball road after missing out on the American League West title, the Rangers weren't supposed to do what they did against the Rays.

They pitched, they hit and they played terrific defense. They played like they had in May and June, when they put themselves in position to even reach the postseason for the first time since 2016.

Tampa Bay didn't stand a chance.

The Rangers finished off a two-game sweep of the Rays, as Nathan Eovaldi allowed one run in 6 2/3 innings and Evan Carter connected for a two-run homer en route to an easy 7-1 victory at Tropicana Field.

With the win, the Rangers advanced AL Division Series against Baltimore.

The Rangers weren't all that chatty about the Orioles, the only AL team to win 100 games (101-61) this season. They enjoyed talking about their wins over the team that won 99 times and posted the league's best home record.

"Just the resilience of at-bats, pitching, competing," shortstop Corey Seager said. "We've never gone down. We've never just gone away and rolled over. To be able to do that in big moments and calm the nerves, it's really special."

Seager collected two doubles but wasn't the story on offense. Carter's homer capped a four-run fourth inning that opened with Adolis García breaking a scoreless tie with a home run and included a Josh Jung blooper that turned into an RBI triple.

Carter hit the next pitch from Zach Eflin out to right-center field.

"He threw the exact same pitch the at-bat before, and I fouled it off," said Carter, who reached in 7 of 8 plate appearances in the series. "I didn't want to miss it again."

Jung also doubled twice. Marcus Semien and Seager delivered back-to-back RBI doubles in the sixth to put the Rangers up 7-0. The other run came in the fifth on a Nathaniel Lowe chopper.

The Rays scored their only run in the series in the seventh, when they pieced together three singles against Eovaldi. He hadn't gone more than five innings since coming off the injured list in September, and he hadn't pitched past six innings since July 1.

He beat the Rays for the third time this year.

"I knew my job today was just go out there and attack the hitters as best as possible and wait until our offense was able to push some runs across the board," Eovaldi said. "And they were able to do that in the fourth inning. From that moment on, it's attack, attack, attack." ∎

Nathan Eovaldi was terrific in the Game 2 win with 6 2/3 innings pitched, one earned run and eight strikeouts.

AMERICAN LEAGUE DIVISION SERIES GAME 1
October 7, 2023 • Baltimore, Maryland
Rangers 3, Orioles 2

RELIEVERS LEAD THE WAY

Sborz-Chapman-Leclerc Trio Holds Orioles Scoreless as Rangers Take Opener

Postseason games aren't supposed to be as one-sided the Rangers made things seem in the American League wild-card round, when they swept two games by a combined 10 runs.

The opener of the AL Division Series was more like it — tight throughout.

Close games weren't a good thing for the Rangers this season, and in Game 1 it sure seemed like the bullpen that had more blown saves than successful saves was trying to give away another against the Orioles.

Instead, the relievers found a way.

Josh Jung homered, Evan Carter delivered an RBI double and Josh Sborz, Aroldis Chapman and José Leclerc managed a scoreless inning apiece as the Rangers held on for a 3-2 victory at Camden Yards.

The relievers needed help from the defense, especially Chapman in the eighth and Leclerc in the ninth. Jung, the rookie third baseman, and All-Star catcher Jonah Heim obliged.

"It got a little bumpy there, but they found a way to get through it," manager Bruce Bochy said.

The victory gives the Rangers home-field advantage in the best-of-5 series.

The Rangers picked lefty Andrew Heaney to start Game 1, even though he would be unable to give them five innings, because the Orioles feature some big left-handed bats and because it's more difficult to hit home runs to left field.

"You've got to get creative, and it worked out well today," Bochy said.

Heaney opened with three scoreless innings and took a 2-0 lead to the mound in the fourth after Carter's double and an RBI single by Heim, but the Orioles got one back with one out in the inning and Dane Dunning replaced Heaney for the final out.

Jung homered in the sixth, but so did Anthony Santander for Orioles. Will Smith was summoned to get Gunnar Henderson to end that inning with the Rangers up 3-2.

Sborz entered for the seventh, and opened with seven straight balls. He recovered, though, to toss a scoreless inning.

Adolis García (53) reaches for the catch in the outfield as his teammate Leody Taveras is also in pursuit.

Chapman was given the eighth, and things looked bleak after he walked the first two Orioles. But Santander hit a bouncer to Jung's left that he turned into a critical double play. Chapman closed the inning with a strikeout of Ryan Mountcastle.

"To take that momentum away was huge," Jung said. "My defense, I just try to take some hits away."

Leclerc, who has cemented his place as the Rangers' closer, gave up a single to Henderson to start the ninth. Henderson tried to steal second base to get into scoring position with no outs, but Heim delivered a perfect throw to Corey Seager for an out that took the wind out of the sellout crowd.

"That was awesome," Jung said. "It was on a changeup, too. He put it right where he needed it."

And where Leclerc needed it. And where the Rangers needed to help them win Game 1.

"It's always good to get the first one," Bochy said. ■

Above: José Leclerc reacts after nailing down the save in the 3-2 Game 1 win over the Orioles. Opposite: Josh Sborz pitched a scoreless seventh inning.

AMERICAN LEAGUE DIVISION SERIES GAME 2
October 8, 2023 • Baltimore, Maryland
Rangers 11, Orioles 8

GRAND GARVER!

Bochy's Lineup Change Proves Key as Rangers Hold on to Take Game 2

Bruce Bochy says lineup decisions for each game are a collaborative effort, with input from his coaching staff, the numbers guys, pro scouts and the front office.

But he is the manager, a three-time World Series-winning manager, and ultimately he's the one who puts pen to paper on the lineup card.

The one he drew up in Game 2 of the American League Division Series was another master stroke.

At long last Mitch Garver returned to the Rangers' lineup in the No. 3 spot, which has been unsettled the past few weeks. It's not unsettled now, as Garver hit a grand slam and drove in five runs as the Rangers sprinted out to a huge lead after three innings and then held on for an 11-8 victory.

Garver just wanted to play after sitting out the Rangers' first three postseason games.

"I was excited," he said. "I feel like anytime I'm in the lineup I can contribute. Whoever's in the lineup that day, I think 1 through 9 we trust everybody to get the job done."

The Rangers returned home from Camden Yards with a 2-0 lead in the best-of-5 series.

Cody Bradford tossed 3 2/3 scoreless innings in relief of fellow left-hander Jordan Montgomery, Corey Seager set an MLB postseason record with five walks, and Leody Taveras scored three runs and got the Rangers started with an RBI double.

They were down 2-0 after one inning, leaving the bases loaded in the first, but scored five times in the second against Orioles rookie Grayson Rodriguez. Taveras brought in the first two and scored his first run as Garver beat out an infield hit that traveled about 30 feet.

"Speed showed up there," Bochy deadpanned.

Garver's next hit went about 400 feet further.

Baltimore's Brian Baker issued three straight walks to Taveras, Marcus Semien and Seager in the third inning before Baker was quickly replaced by Jacob Webb. He fell behind Garver 3-1, and with the bases loaded Garver figured that Webb was going to throw a fastball.

He did, and Garver hit it 419 feet for the second grand slam in Rangers postseason history.

"These playoff games, it's one swing can change it," Garver said. "I got into a situation there in a hitter's count where I was looking for a fastball, and I got it."

Catcher Jonah Heim and closer José Leclerc celebrate after finishing out the 11-8 win over Baltimore.

Garver didn't complain that he hadn't played. Instead, he said that Bochy's pedigree is ironclad. The decision to insert Garver was the second big decision of the series, after the Rangers went with left-hander Andrew Heaney to start Game 1 instead of the well-rested Dane Dunning.

"I think the decisions he makes when it comes to the bullpen and the lineup, nobody can argue with them just based on his resume," Garver said. "We trust his decisions."

Bochy was rewarded but didn't get the rest of the day off after Garver put the Rangers up 9-2.

Montgomery labored and had to exit in the fifth after the Orioles cut the Rangers' lead to 10-5. Bradford, another crafty lefty, turned in one of the more memorable middle-relief appearances in Rangers postseason history, along with Derek Holland's outing in Game 3 of the 2010 AL Championship Series.

Josh Sborz recorded the final out in the eighth, needing only one pitch after consecutive hits against Bradford, and the Rangers went with Brock Burke in the ninth with an 11-5 lead. He got one out but exited after allowing a walk and a hit, and José Leclerc allowed a three-run homer to Aaron Hicks.

That was it, though, as the Rangers won their fourth straight postseason game.

Credit the manager and Garver.

"He came up big earlier, too, with that swinging bunt," Bochy said. "He can hit, and he's done a great job for us this year. He got a pitch he could handle, and he's got big power. That was the difference in the game." ■

Mitch Garver connects on a grand slam, part of a huge Game 2 that saw him collect two hits and five RBI.

AMERICAN LEAGUE DIVISION SERIES GAME 3

October 10, 2023 • Arlington, Texas

Rangers 7, Orioles 1

PITCH (CLOCK) PERFECT

Floodgates Open After Lowe's 15-Pitch At-Bat as Rangers Complete Sweep

The inning-by-inning summary at mlb.com for Game 3 of the American League Championship Series shows that Nathaniel Lowe lined out to left field to open the second inning.

Click on the outcome, though, and a much different story emerges.

The Rangers first baseman saw 15 pitches from Orioles right-hander Dean Kremer. In the age of the pitch clock, they had no choice but to keep attacking each other.

"I ran out of gas there pretty early," Lowe said.

What he didn't know then, but what his teammates and manager Bruce Bochy thought, is that he had just delivered the at-bat of the game.

Five runs would follow in the inning, with Adolis García capping the rally with a three-run homer that sent the Rangers on their way to a 7-1 victory over the Orioles and a three-game sweep of the ALDS.

"I think that was a key at-bat in the game," García said. "It was a moment we were able to see a lot of pitches from the pitcher, just being able to stretch that out and us take advantage of that. I think it was a great at-bat."

Josh Jung hit the next pitch after Lowe's marathon at-bat for a single, and Marcus Semien doubled two batters later. The Orioles opted to walk Corey Seager, a decision that loaded the bases for Mitch Garver.

He didn't hit a grand slam, as he did in Game 2, but he brought in two with a double past third base and kept the inning going for García.

"You definitely saw less quality pitches after that [Lowe] at-bat," Semien said. "That's what our philosophy is all about. Make the pitcher work. Make it hard on him. Obviously, it a road game for him and a tough environment, so anything we could do to make it tough on him we did. Nate didn't get a base hit, but he did get everything rolling."

After going to a full count on the seventh pitch, Lowe fouled off seven consecutive pitches. The sellout crowd of 40,861 cheered louder with each ball into the stands. Lowe had used his timeout, and Kremer just kept pumping.

Were there not a pitch clock, he might have stepped of the rubber a few times and Lowe might have stepped out of the batter's box.

Seager and Garver, who were four and five batters away from hitting in the inning, saw the toll the at-bat took on Kremer.

"We got done with that, and I remember turning to Corey, and he was like, 'Hey, this guy's breathing hard,'"

Nathan Eovaldi was once again dominant in a close-out game, tossing seven innings with seven strikeouts while only allowing one run.

Garver said. "Sure enough, man, we put the pressure on him, and he had to come in the zone."

Lowe might have also turned his fortunes around. He entered Tuesday only 20 for 122 (.164) in his past 33 games, but he made a hard out on the 15th pitch and connected for a home run in the sixth.

As the ball sailed into the seats, the relief he felt was plain to see as he took a breath and pumped both fists before making his trot around the bases. Not only has Lowe been struggling at the plate, his mother is also battling brain cancer.

"We were excited for him," manager Bruce Bochy said. "He's dealing with a lot right now, been battling it at the plate. To hit the home run, I think you could see a sense of relief, like, 'I'm back.' But he felt good before the game. Sure enough, he goes out there and hits a home run." ∎

Above: The Rangers stayed perfect in the postseason and celebrated clinching a berth in the ALCS. Opposite: Reliever Aroldis Chapman got two outs in the eighth inning as the Rangers prevailed in Game 3, 7-1.

AMERICAN LEAGUE CHAMPIONSHIP SERIES GAME 1
October 15, 2023 · Houston, Texas
Rangers 2, Astros 0

CHALLENGE ACCEPTED

Evan Carter Catch, Jose Altuve Gaffe Help Rangers Take Game 1 of ALCS

Marcus Semien saw it the whole way. Corey Seager saw it, too.

The entire Rangers bench also knew in the eighth inning Sunday that Jose Altuve didn't properly retouch second base as he returned to first following a leaping catch by Evan Carter at the left-field wall.

Even Altuve knew.

"He was pretty beside himself at first base," first baseman Nathaniel Lowe said.

The only one who didn't know was second-base umpire Doug Eddings, who was watching the catch, didn't see Altuve's return path and called him safe. The Rangers challenged without hesitation, and the replay ump didn't miss it.

The Altuve miscue was the play of Game 1, which the Rangers won 2-0 at Minute Maid Park to open the best-of-7 American League Championship Series.

"That's a play where I always watch to see what the runner does," Semien said. "Sometimes the umpires are looking at the ball, and that's exactly what Doug told me. But, luckily, that's a play we can review."

Altuve started the eighth with a walk from Josh Sborz, who was quickly replaced by the human rollercoaster ride, Aroldis Chapman. Alex Bregman was next, and he sent a towering drive into left field near the 366-foot sigh in front of the Rangers' bullpen.

Carter jumped, extended his left arm and came down with the ball. Altuve, thinking the ball might hit off the wall or land in the seats, aggressively went to second base, touching it and shuffling in front of the base and returning to first. The rule states that a runner must touch the bag again on his way back to first.

Semien pointed out Altuve's gaffe as it happened.

"Thank goodness for replay," pitching coach Mike Maddux said.

Eddings' call was overturned, and suddenly the bases were empty with two outs instead of a runner on first with Yordan Alvarez and José Abreu coming to bat against Chapman. He got Alvarez to tap softly to first base, and José Leclerc tossed a perfect ninth to close out the Rangers' sixth straight victory to open the postseason.

"That was a crazy play where that could have been a home run or an extra-base hit, and we end up getting two outs," Semien said.

The events of the eighth inning overshadowed the performance of left-hander Jordan Montgomery, who tossed 6 1/3 scoreless innings. Leody Taveras homered off

Evan Carter makes a leaping catch to rob the Houston Astros' Alex Bregman of a hit during the eighth inning of ALCS Game 1 at Minute Maid Park.

of Justin Verlander, and Carter had a hand in two terrific catches and also legged out a second-inning double to set up the Rangers' first run.

Carter had never played at Minute Maid Park, which has a peculiar left field featuring the Crawford Boxes only 315 feet away, an old-fashioned out-of-town scoreboard that can produce funky hops and the cranny where Carter made his catch.

He said that outfielder Robbie Grossman, who played early in his career for the Astros, and outfield instructor Will Venable showed him the ropes Saturday during the Rangers' workout.

"The kid Carter, what a game he had out there," manager Bruce Bochy said.

The Rangers did just enough against Verlander, who left the bases loaded in the second after Jonah Heim brought in Carter and Josh Jung and Taveras walked. Verlander retired eight in a row before Taveras' first career postseason homer in the fifth.

The Astros had just missed two-out chances in the third and fourth against Montgomery, who escaped the third by striking out Alvarez. Montgomery struck out the weak-hitting Martín Maldonado with the bases loaded to end the fourth.

Of Montgomery's six strikeouts, three of them were of Alvarez.

"He's a really good hitter, so you have to do a little bit of everything to him," Montgomery said. "We worked the fastball in and out and threw some curveballs for strikes and expanded and made some big pitches when we needed to."

The Rangers will turn to right-hander Nathan Eovaldi on Monday with the opportunity to take both road games to open the series before potentially playing three games at Globe Life Field.

"Game 1 is important because we're on the road," Semien said. "We get three games at home, but our focus is not on that. Our focus is on tomorrow." ■

Jonah Heim hits an RBI single during the second inning to drive in Evan Carter. Leody Taveras would later add to the Rangers' scoring with a solo home run.

AMERICAN LEAGUE CHAMPIONSHIP SERIES GAME 2
October 16, 2023 • Houston, Texas
Rangers 5, Astros 4

THE GREAT ESCAPE

Eovaldi, Rangers Survive Game 2, Head Home with 2-0 ALCS Lead

Nothing matters this time of year besides winning, and the Texas Rangers have become masters of that in the MLB postseason.

Any possible way to win a ballgame, the Rangers have done it.

Maybe it hasn't been pretty and maybe fingernails are being chewed and heads of hair are turning gray, but no one has beaten the Rangers in their seven playoff games.

As nerve-racking as things became Monday afternoon and into the evening, the Rangers once again found a way.

Now, they find themselves in the driver's seat in the American League Championship Series.

The Rangers scored four times in the first inning of Game 2, then sweated out the final two innings en route to a 5-4 victory at Minute Maid Park that gave them a 2-0 lead in the best-of-7 series against the rival Astros.

Game 3 is at Globe Life Field, and right-hander Max Scherzer is expected to start for the Rangers. They know the series isn't over, but they also know that they have an enormous leg up after capturing the first two games on the road.

"That's what we came here for," first baseman Nathaniel Lowe said. "We got two chances to compete and came away with two Ws. We've got some good momentum going into an off day. The crowd's going to be behind us at home, and you saw with the last series we had really good energy at home. We like our chances going forward."

The biggest sequence in the game wasn't José Leclerc wiggling out of an eighth-inning jam before working a perfect ninth inning, though that might have been when Metroplex heart rates peaked.

Three innings earlier, though, Nathan Eovaldi pulled a great escape after the Astros loaded the bases with no outs but failed to score.

The Rangers were leading 5-2 when consecutive singles and a Josh Jung error on a slow bouncer gave the Astros their best chance of the game. They went to pinch hitter Yainer Diaz, an offensive upgrade over Martín Maldonado, but Eovaldi struck him out to end a six-pitch at-bat.

Jose Altuve was next, and Eovaldi got him swinging, too. Alex Bregman, who homered in the fourth, followed but hit a chopper to Jung two pitches later.

Eovaldi said the key against Diaz was making him chase off the plate, and he had set up Altuve during their earlier at-bats.

"You're close, but you're not out of the woods yet because Bregman is equally as talented," Eovaldi said.

Getting Bregman, whose homer clanged off the left-

Starting pitcher Nathan Eovaldi escaped tight jams across six innings as the Rangers held on to beat the Astros.

field foul pole, was just a matter of making a good pitch.

"That was the turning point in the game," manager Bruce Bochy said.

The Astros added another run in the sixth, and Yordan Alvarez hit his second homer of the game with two outs in the eighth against Aroldis Chapman. Bochy summoned José Leclerc from the bullpen, and he promptly walked José Abreu and Michael Brantley.

Chas McCormick, though, hit a bouncer to Jung, and the Rangers were out of the inning.

"I felt a little accelerated in the eighth," said Leclerc, who has pitched in all seven postseason games. "I didn't have my best stuff, either, but I just tried to compete with what I had."

The Rangers opened the game with singles from Marcus Semien and Corey Seager on the first two pitches from Framber Valdez, and Semien scored as Valdez chucked the ball into foul territory behind first base after bobbling a Robbie Grossman tapper near the third-base line.

Adolis García and Mitch Garver followed with RBI singles, and the Ranges were up 3-0 before Valdez recorded an out. Lowe singled two batters later for a 4-0 lead.

Alvarez connected off of Eovaldi in the second, but Jonah Heim countered that in the third with a shot to left field.

And, then, the Rangers stopped scoring. The Astros' terrific bullpen had a hand in that, as five relievers held the Rangers to one hit over the final 6 1/3 innings.

Their performance was almost good enough. The Rangers, though, found a way to win yet again, and now they are two wins away from playing in their third World Series.

"The momentum is in our favor, but we can't let the guard down," Eovaldi said. "The Astros are an incredible team, and they have the lineup from top to bottom and they have good pitching. We've got to keep doing what we've been doing and bring this momentum back home to Arlington." ■

Jonah Heim greets Rangers teammates in the dugout after hitting a home run during the third inning in Houston.

AMERICAN LEAGUE CHAMPIONSHIP SERIES GAME 3
October 18, 2023 • Arlington, Texas
Astros 8, Rangers 5

IMPERFECT

Rangers Lose First Postseason Game as Max Scherzer Falters

The Rangers knew that what happened Wednesday night was a possibility.

Max Scherzer knew it, too.

He was coming off the injured list and pitching for the first time since Sept. 12. Yeah, he threw a couple of simulated games, in empty ballparks against hitters from his own team and felt good about them, but they couldn't match the intensity of a postseason game.

A pitcher needs to be at his best in October, and at times Scherzer was. Ultimately, though, he pitched like a guy who hadn't been on a mound in more than a month.

The result was five Astros runs against him in four innings and an 8-5 Rangers loss that gave the Astros life in the American League Championship Series. The Rangers still hold a 2-1 lead in the best-of-7 series, which continues with Game 4 at Globe Life Field.

"They got to me," Scherzer said. "It was just execution and mistakes."

Josh Jung swatted two two-run homers for the Rangers, who were no-hit into the fifth inning by Cristian Javier. Leody Taveras made the best play so far of the MLB postseason when he made a leaping catch in center field to rob Astros menace Yordan Alvarez of a homer to start the sixth inning.

Evan Carter, in his first game as the Rangers' No. 3 hitter, collected a sixth-inning double, but that was his only hit in four at-bats. Adolis García had the only other RBI for the Rangers with a single in the eighth.

The Rangers were out-hit, though, 12-6.

"We knew coming in we had our hands full," manager Bruce Bochy said.

Scherzer wasn't terrible. He had good zip on his fastball, and Astros hitters swung through several of his curveballs. But he made the mistakes that a rusty pitcher is prone to make, like hitting a batter in an 0-2 count and leaving too many pitches over the heart of the plate.

"There's some bad in this, I get it," Scherzer said. "That's where you have to tune out and look at the good. What did I do well? I made some mistakes, I get it, and I got punished for it, but there were some good things I also did as well. It's tough to take a loss in the postseason any time, but I'm not going to sit here and beat myself down."

He hit Alvarez to start the second and compounded that with a one-out walk. After a single loaded the bases, Scherzer retired Jeremy Peña to bring up No. 9 hitter Martín Maldonado. Things looked promising, but a wild pitch allowed Alvarez to score the game's first run and Maldonado collected a two-run single for a 3-0 lead.

Jose Altuve homered to start the third, and the Astros went double, groundout, single for another run in the fourth.

Bochy said that the Rangers were not second-guessing their decision to start Scherzer.

"He's one of our guys," Bochy said. "There's no regret on that."

Astros center fielder Mauricio Dubón scores during the second inning as Jonah Heim reaches for the throw. Starter Max Scherzer allowed five runs in his first outing back from injury.

The Rangers hadn't even collected a hit by the time Scherzer exited.

They final did with two outs in the fifth as Nathaniel Lowe singled to left field. Jung followed with his first two-run homer, but the Rangers couldn't any closer than three the rest of the way against Javier and three Astros relievers.

"They've got a really good staff," Jung said. "You're not going to go out there and score seven runs every game. That's probably our first scuffle. That's baseball."

Left-hander Andrew Heaney will start Game 4 for the Rangers, who could use right-hander Dane Dunning in a piggyback system that helped them win Game 1 of the division series at Baltimore. Neither has pitched since, though both warmed up Monday during Game 2.

The Rangers did not use their key bullpen arms, including closer José Leclerc for the first time this postseason, and should be reloaded in the late innings if they can get there with a lead.

They have no doubt they will bounce back in Game 4.

"It's something we've done pretty much all season," Jung said. "We are where we are because of our resilience." ■

AMERICAN LEAGUE CHAMPIONSHIP SERIES GAME 4
October 19, 2023 • Arlington, Texas
Astros 10, Rangers 3

REELING

Astros Pull Even in ACLS with Game 4 Rout of Rangers

The best-of-7 American League Championship Series is now a best-of-3, and the Rangers are reeling.

They dropped their second consecutive game Thursday night, losing 10-3 in Game 4 to fall into a tie with the Astros at two games apiece. Houston started fasted and didn't flinch after the Rangers erased an early 3-0 deficit.

The Rangers' pitching did them in again, this time as starter Andrew Heaney couldn't finish the first inning and as Dane Dunning allowed three of the four runs in the Astros' fourth. The big blow was a three-run homer by José Abreu against left-hander Cody Bradford with two outs, but the two walks issued by Dunning to start the inning, after the Rangers had just tied the game, put the wheels in motion.

"In a situation where we needed a shutdown inning, I didn't do it," Dunning said. "I didn't do my job."

The good news for the Rangers is that left-hander Jordan Montgomery will start Game 5. The bad news is that he will be opposed by right-hander Justin Verlander while having to shut down an Astros offense that can't stop scoring runs at Globe Life Field.

Dating to July, the Astros have won seven straight games here while outscoring the Rangers 74-32. The series is guaranteed to return to Minute Maid Park on Sunday for Game 6, and that might be a good thing.

"They have played well in this ballpark, and we have to stop that," Bruce Bochy said.

Adolis García and Corey Seager hit solo homers for the Rangers. Seager's shot to start the third pulled the Rangers into a 3-3 tie that didn't last an inning as Dunning unraveled.

He walked No. 9 hitter Martín Maldonado to start the fourth, his biggest sin in the inning, and then walked Jose Altuve before a Maurico Dubón single loaded the bases with no outs.

Dunning struck out Alex Bregman, but Bochy went to Bradford for a left-on-left matchup against Yordan Alvarez. The Rangers dodged a bullet as Alvarez's just missed a home run, settling for a sacrifice fly, but Bradford missed his spot on his sixth pitch to Abreu.

Abreu didn't miss it.

Dunning knew afterward how costly the leadoff walk to Maldonado, who is batting .182 this postseason, became.

"In a situation like that, I've got to be in the zone more," Dunning said. "It's frustrating. He's ninth in the lineup for a reason, and I walked him. You bring up the top of the order with Altuve with a runner on, I'm trying to get a double play and just missed with a couple changeups and an uncompetitive 3-1 sinker."

The Astros' relievers stifled the Rangers once again after the early offense, as they did in Game 1 and Game 2.

Second baseman Marcus Semien is tagged out by José Abreu while diving back to first base during a lopsided Game 4.

The Rangers had only three hits the rest of the way, the first two coming in the fifth as Leody Taveras and Marcus Semien opened with singles.

Seager was next, and he hit a 108.6-mph line drive to first that Abreu snagged and then tagged the batting glove sticking out of Semien's back pocket for a rally-killing double play.

"It's a good play by Abreu," Semien said. "I didn't feel a tag. I've been putting my gloves in my back pocket my entire career, and that's the first time that's happened."

But bad luck didn't doom the Rangers.

The pitching did, and the best-of-7 ALCS is now a best-of-3.

"I always like my chances with this club," Bochy said. "They've battled all year. We're playing a good team. Nobody thought this was going to be easy. We've been in this kind of situation where we've had to bounce back, and that's what we need to do." ■

AMERICAN LEAGUE CHAMPIONSHIP SERIES GAME 5
October 20, 2023 · Arlington, Texas
Astros 5, Rangers 4

ON THE ROPES

Jose Altuve's Late Homer Lifts Astros Past Rangers After Tempers Rise in Game 5

Facing a critical game Friday afternoon, the Rangers showed fight.

And then they nearly fought.

And then they were knocked to the canvas.

The Rangers have one day to recover from Jose Altuve's ninth-inning, three-run homer that sent the Astros to a 5-4 Game 5 victory and vaulted him into a 3-2 lead in the American League Championship Series.

Game 6 will be at Minute Maid Park, and the Rangers have to win to keep their season alive.

"It's just a tough one, no getting around it," manager Bruce Bochy said. "It's part of the game and what you have to deal with, and good clubs deal with it the right way. These guys, they'll put this behind them."

Altuve's go-ahead blast came moments after the benches cleared following Adolis García getting plunked in the eighth inning on the first pitch of his first at-bat after hitting a three-run homer that gave the Rangers a 4-2 lead.

García confronted Astros catcher Martín Maldonado, who has been in the middle of past tensions between the Rangers and Astros and had to be held back as players flooded onto the field. García and right-hander Bryan Abreu were ejected, as was Astros manager Dusty Baker for arguing the umpires' decision to toss Abreu.

"I just reacted to the ball that came toward me," García said. "In that situation he could have hurt me, and it's something I let him know that shouldn't happen. It was just the heat of the moment."

The Astros and Rangers were tied at 1 after five innings, after an exchange of homers by Alex Bregman and Nathaniel Lowe. Houston reclaimed a one-run lead in the sixth as Bregman scored on José Abreu single that short-hopped Corey Seager at shortstop.

Had he fielded the ball cleanly, he could have turned an inning-ending double play that would have kept the Astros from scoring.

Seager responded in the Rangers' sixth with a one-out double. Evan Carter followed with a single that move Seager to third for García, who's high flyball carried just behind the left-field wall.

García spiked his bat and celebrated on his way to first base, which the Rangers believe led to García getting hit in the eighth. Verlander, for his part, said that he was not upset with García's reaction.

"I don't think anybody is mad about him pimping a homer," Verlander said. "It was the biggest homer in his career, quite honestly."

After eight innings, it looked as if García's blast would

The Houston Astros and Texas Rangers cleared the benches in Game 5 after the Rangers' Adolis García was hit by a pitch thrown by relief pitcher Bryan Abreu during the eighth inning.

be a knockout blow for the Rangers. But the ensuing delay to settle the fracas might have frozen closer José Leclerc, who recorded the final out of the Astros' eighth, while potentially lighting a fire under the Astros.

Leclerc allowed a leadoff single to pinch-hitter Yainer Diaz and walked pinch-hitter Jon Singleton before Altuve's blast.

The first two Rangers reached in the ninth, but Ryan Pressly shut the door and put the Rangers on the brink.

"It's up to us to respond now," said second baseman Marcus Semien, who lined out for the first out of the ninth. "The season's on the line. That's a building we've played good baseball in. Let's continue to do that. That's all we can try to do." ∎

AMERICAN LEAGUE CHAMPIONSHIP SERIES GAME 6
October 22, 2023 · Houston, Texas
Rangers 9, Astros 2

BOUNCE BACK

Rangers Force Game 7 with Clutch Late-Inning Performances by Leclerc, García

Big Game Nate Eovaldi gave the Rangers a chance Sunday night.

So did Jonah Heim and Mitch Garver.

Even the struggling Marcus Semien reached base four times.

Still, the Rangers' season came down to the bullpen and a locally reviled slugger who had struck out in his first four at-bats.

See you for Game 7.

José Leclerc, two days after blowing the save in a gut-wrenching Game 5 loss, pitched the Rangers out of a major jam in the eighth, and Adolis García hit a ninth-inning grand slam in a 9-2 victory that forced a winner-take-all game in the American League Championship Series.

The Rangers, who will give Max Scherzer his second start of the series in the finale, might have been the only ones at Minute Maid Park who believed there would be a Game 7.

"During the season we've had our ups and downs," manager Bruce Bochy said. "We've had some tough streaks, injuries. But these guys keep getting up and they keep bouncing back.

"It's about being resilient in this game because it doesn't matter if it happens or not, it's more how you handle it. And so these guys have done a great job of putting that behind them and tough loss in Game 5."

Heim hit a two-run homer, and Garver homered and collected and RBI double in the eighth that gave the Rangers a 4-2 lead. Josh Sborz, who induced a critical double play to end the seventh inning after Eovaldi exited, walked Alex Bregman to open the eighth but stuck out Yordan Alvarez.

After a José Abreu single, Leclerc replaced Sborz with two on, one out and All-Star Kyle Tucker batting as the potential go-ahead run. Tucker has struggled throughout the postseason, but Leclerc said that the Rangers wanted to be careful with him. Tucker walked to load the bases.

That brought Mauricio Dubón, who had made it 3-2 in the sixth with a sacrifice fly. This time, though, he hit a soft liner to shortstop Corey Seager.

The Astros went to pinch-hitter Jon Singleton, a left-handed batter, for a more favorable matchup against the right-handed Leclerc. Singleton worked a full count, fouled off two pitches but swung through a Leclerc cutter to go down swinging.

Forty-eight hours after the costliest blown save of his career, Leclerc said he was as confident as ever.

"I went ought there and thought, 'I have the ability to get guys out,'" he said. "I was just trying to follow the plan and execute, and I trust my stuff."

The escape might have given the Rangers life or taken

José Leclerc rebounded from a blown save the previous night to keep the Rangers' hopes alive in Game 6.

some starch out of the Astros. Josh Jung drew a leadoff walk from Rafael Montero to start the ninth, and Leody Taveras was safe after Jose Altuve bobbled a high hopper.

Semien followed with a single to load the bases for Corey Seager, who was credited with a painful RBI after a Ryne Stanek pitch hit him in the leg. Stanek, though, recovered to strike out Evan Carter.

García was next. Astros fans had booed him loudly for each pitch after he sparked a benches-clearing scuffle in Game 5 and then avoided being suspended by MLB. This at-bat was no different.

Stanek blew a 97-mph heater past García but missed inside to even the count. Stanek's next pitch came in at 97.4 mph and left García's bat at 110.1 mph.

The line drive found the Crawford Boxes, which would empty rather quickly with the Rangers suddenly up by seven.

"That was a lot of fun," Seager said. "This team's been resilient all year. I didn't expect anything to change tonight."

The Astros jumped on Eovaldi early, making him throw 25 pitches in the first inning. Alvarez knocked in a run with one out after Altuve singled and Michael Brantley walked to start the inning.

Garver quickly tied the game with a homer on the first pitch of the second inning, and the game stayed tied at 1 until the fourth. Garver singled with two outs to keep the inning alive for Heim, who lofted his second homer of the series against Framber Valdez.

It wasn't the deepest home run Heim has ever hit, at just 336 feet, and it was mildly surprising that right fielder Kyle Tucker didn't come down with it.

He might have if it had gone 335 feet.

"I was really blowing really hard to get some wind going," Heim said. "The amount of relief in my body was great."

So was the relief the Rangers felt after extending their season, but they weren't celebrating. They know they have work to do in Game 7.

"It's one game to settle it all, and I think everyone is excited for that," Garver said. ∎

Mitch Garver celebrates after hitting a home run during the second inning of Game 6. Garver opened the scoring for the Rangers in what turned into a 9-2 rout of the Astros.

AMERICAN LEAGUE CHAMPIONSHIP SERIES GAME 7
October 23, 2023 · Houston, Texas
Rangers 11, Astros 4

NO MORE HEARTBREAK

Game 7 Rout Sends Rangers to Third World Series in Club History

No matter how many early runs they scored, no matter how big their cushion over the Astros became or who was pitching, the only thing that was going to allow the Rangers to breathe easy was the 27th out.

These are the Rangers, for whom heartbreak has been hiding just around the corner since 2011. Hell, heartbreak has been a member of their bullpen much of this season.

And they were playing the Astros, the reigning world champions and the Rangers' kryptonite much of the past seven years. Yes, they were terrible at home this season, but their lineup can put up runs in bunches.

No one knows that better than the Rangers.

The 27th out finally came, more than three hours after Game 7 of the American League Championship Series started, and the Rangers' hearts are still beating.

They are headed to the World Series.

Adolis García homered twice and drove in five runs, and Corey Seager and Nathaniel Lowe also homered as the Rangers rolled to an 11-4 victory to win the third American League pennant in club history.

"This team has played with so much heart and determination as any club I've had," manager Bruce Bochy said. "It's just amazing how they kept getting up. We went through ups and downs with the injuries. We ran into a lot of streaks. To come in here and do this shows you how determined they were to find a way."

García, with five home runs and 15 RBIs, was the easy choice for ALCS MVP after setting the MLB record for most RBIs in any postseason series. Josh Hamilton and Nelson Cruz were ALCS MVPs in 2010 and 2011.

García was booed lustily in Game 6 for his involvement in a benches-clearing shoving match in Game 5. After striking out in his first four at-bats in Game 6, he connected for a grand slam that ensured a Game 7.

He collected four more RBIs in his first four at-bats Monday.

"You can't really deny that October has that type of emotion, has that type of situation around it," he said. "I just try to keep myself focused on the task at hand, try to perform, try to control the things that I can, and have the success that we can have."

After he connected for his second homer, he cupped his ear as if to ask the Minute Maid Park crowd to let him hear some more.

"When there's a lot of emotions, the fans out there, they are rallying for their team, it fuels me," García said. "It's motivation that helps me out when I'm playing."

Adolis García hits his first of two home runs in Game 7. García was named ALCS MVP after setting the MLB record for most RBIs in any postseason series.

Seager's home run in the first inning against Cristian Javier traveled 440 feet with an exit velocity of 113.1 mph and landed in the second deck in right field. He also doubled and added a single in the Rangers' four-run fourth.

It wasn't so much his third home run of the postseason that sparked the rest of team, but his reaction to it.

"He does show emotion, but he really showed it when he came in," Bochy said. "He fired up the whole club. That seemed like it just got us going. And it got contagious. I have to credit with him what happened early in that ballgame, in the whole game, how excited he was and how fired up he got the whole club."

Jordan Montgomery was credited with his second win of the series after 2 1/3 scoreless innings in relief of Max Scherzer, who started and allowed two runs in 2 2/3 innings. The Rangers knew they would have Montgomery available and would turn to him when the moment called for it.

With a left-handed hitter coming to face Scherzer with a runner at third, Montgomery got the call.

"Monty, the hot hand, gave us all he had," pitching coach Mike Maddux said. "Monty's been a best, and having him available, that's the guy we've got to go with."

The Rangers have won all eight of their road games this postseason, including four against the Astros in just the second postseason series in MLB history in which the home team failed to win a game.

Now, the Rangers are going to the World Series. ■

The Texas Rangers celebrate their victory over the Houston Astros to secure a spot in the World Series. The Rangers won 11-4 in Game 7.